THINK AND BE PHENOMENAL

THE 5 LEVELS OF BEING PHENOMENAL

HOWARD PARTRIDGE

Published by Motivational Press, Inc.
7777 N Wickham Rd, # 12-247
Melbourne, FL 32940
www.MotivationalPress.com

Manufactured in the United States of America.

ISBN: 978-1-62865-114-0

Contents

Dedication

To our phenomenal son Christian…

Thank you for helping me <u>become</u> a better person

Acknowledgements

To my early mentors, Dr. Ralph W. Neighbour Jr. for introducing me to this concept and Dr. William A. Beckham for helping me learn about true values.

"Who Do You Think You Are?"

Several years ago, I was part of a small group of local service company owners who met every week to network. Many in this group had what Zig Ziglar calls "Stinkin' Thinkin'" and needed a "check-up-from-the-neck-up" - it left them with a serious case of "hardening of the attitudes"!

They complained about the economy and whined that customers wouldn't pay their prices. They were disgusted because they didn't have much business.

As they complained, I couldn't help but notice how some of them were dressed - cut-off blue jeans, flip-flops and they hadn't shaven. I arrived every week wearing a sport coat, a tie, and a positive attitude. They laughed at me and said, "Who do you think you are, Zig Ziglar or somebody?"

The funny thing is I didn't know Zig at the time; I had never met him at that point. Today, I'm the exclusive small business coach for the Ziglar Inc., Zig has appeared at my conferences and Tom Ziglar (Zig's son) and I have done over 50 speaking engagements together around the world including Cambridge University. The last chapter of Zig's very *last* book , *BORN TO WIN,* was based on one of my teachings.

The irony is that the most important thing I learned from Zig Ziglar is this...

Who you THINK you are and what you think you can do will have the biggest impact on your success in life and business

The image you have of yourself determines the success you have in life and business. What you THINK about your *potential* for success will make the biggest difference in your *actual* success. What you THINK about God and what you THINK about others literally affects the actions you take, which ultimately determines your success. When we connect *how we think* to our habits that control us, everything changes.

This book takes you through the process everyone goes through when attempting to change a habit, learn a new skill or implement a new idea.

It all starts with how you THINK of yourself.

Zig taught that a poor self-image is what keeps humans from the success they were created to have. What we truly believe about ourselves limits our potential because every human acts or doesn't act based on how they see themselves. You will take action based on the *picture* you see in your mind. So, you must change the picture if you want to change your results.

You may not even be aware of your limiting thoughts because they are often hidden in what I call the *conditioned identity*. Your conditioned identity is the image that you've accepted of yourself based on the *conditioning* you have received over a lifetime of input.

We are told what we can and can't do by family members, society and the media. We are placed in a box by others' wishes rather than living out the true purpose we were created for.

"This is just who I am" is often the motto.

This book is about discovering how to BE the phenomenal person you were created to BE, so that you will DO the phenomenal things you are supposed to do and HAVE the phenomenal life you are meant to have.

This book is about living out of your *position* rather than your *condition*. Every human has a position that is misunderstood. When I meet a stranger, and we exchange "How are you?," I always say "phenomenal," of course. And I follow with "And so are you!" The responses I get from that vary from "Well, thank you," to "I know!" to "What do you mean?"

Then I ask this crucial question: "Do you know WHY you are phenomenal? Do you believe in God?" (Most say yes). "Well, God don't make no junk right? Everything He makes is phenomenal!"

We weren't created to be unsuccessful, were we? The problem is that we don't know that we ARE created to be phenomenal, and therefore don't act accordingly. This book is about the processes of becoming who you already are. How ironic.

Zig said…

*You are **WHAT** you are and **WHERE** you are because of what has gone into your mind. You can **CHANGE** what you are and where you are by **CHANGING** what goes into your mind.*

Frank Outlaw said….

*When you Change your **THINKING**,*
*You Change your **BELIEFS**.*

When you Change your beliefs,
*You Change your **EXPECTATIONS**.*

When you Change your expectations,
*You Change your **ATTITUDE**.*

When you Change your attitude,
*You Change your **BEHAVIOR**.*

When you Change your behavior,
*You Change your **PERFORMANCE**.*

When you Change your performance
*You Change your **LIFE***

He also said…

*Watch your **THOUGHTS**, they become **WORDS***
*Watch your words, they become **ACTIONS***
*Watch your actions, they become **HABITS***
*Watch your habits, they become your **CHARACTER***
*Watch your character, they determine your **DESTINY***

In *As a Man Thinketh*, James Allen says, "A man is literally *what he thinks*, his character being the complete sum of all his thoughts."

The 5 Levels of BEing Phenomenal

Zig said, "You have to *be* before you can *do*, and you have to *do* before you can *have*." If you want to *have* a different life, a different business or different habits you obviously have to *do* some things differently. Zig says, "You will not *consistently* do *inconsistently* with how you see yourself. The only way to consistently *do* things differently is to *BEcome* a different person, and to see yourself as such."

Stephen R. Covey said in his classic book, *The 7 Habits of Highly Effective People,* "We need a new level, a deeper level of thinking… this new level of thinking is a principle-centered, character-based, "inside-out" approach… which means to start first with self; even more fundamentally, to start with the most *inside* part of self – with your paradigms, your character, and your motives. It says if you want to *have* a happy marriage, *be* the kind of person who generates positive energy… if you want to *have* more freedom in your job, *be* a more responsible, a more helpful, a more contributing employee…"

The 5 Levels of BEing Phenomenal is a process all humans go through as we attempt to develop new habits. These steps take you from *thinking* about a new idea to the process of creating new habits. It happens faster or slower for some, depending on a number of factors.

I call them "levels" because you reach a new level of "being" at each stage. You could call them steps or stages as well. By understanding the five levels of being, you'll be able to assess where you are in the process. You'll be able to recognize if you're making progress, getting stuck, or sliding backward.

Notice: This is NOT a new age, regurgitated Law of Attraction book! Yes, everything starts with thinking, but you do have to *do* something and that's called the Law of Action!

The 2 Reasons I Wrote This Book…

The first reason is most people don't know *who* they are. They don't realize their potential and don't understand they can do more than they think. Henry Ford said, "If you think you *can* or you think you can't, you're right."

John Maxwell says, "The difference between highly successful people and those who aren't is how they *think* (and what they think about)." Earl Nightingale said, "*All* the prophets agree on this one thing – you become what you think."

The second reason I wrote this book: As I taught *The 5 Levels* to my business coaching clients over the years, it has gotten more positive response than any other subject I've taught. I get more positive feedback and more "aha" moments with this teaching than any other.

Although my business training has revolutionized small businesses around the world, *The 5 Levels* generate such a positive response because we *know* that in order to build a phenomenally successful business, we must *become* a phenomenally successful person.

The 5 Levels also generate a lot of interest because it reveals the *process* we all go through when we attempt to change our habits, learn a new skill, or implement a new idea. So, I decided to get this message in print so that more people could have access to it. I first learned the five levels from one of my early mentors, Dr. Ralph Neighbour, Jr. Although he called them "filters," you could also call them stages or levels.

The goal of this book is to bring awareness to the *process* of change – *The 5 Levels* everyone goes through as you attempt to change your habits, learn a new skill or implement a new idea. When you're in tune with what is happening in your mind, will and emotion, you're more likely to be successful. Many people give up because they don't understand the process of change. This book walks you through the process, so that you can harness the power of it.

In addition to *The 5 Levels*, I'll share a few nuggets on setting goals. Without a meaningful goal, the process is just a muse. It's just an interesting exercise if you don't attach it to a goal. On the other hand, you will not be able to reach new dreams and new goals without going through *The 5 Levels*. No one does.

You will not BEcome the person you were created to be spiritually, mentally, emotionally or physically without going through *The 5 Levels* process. You won't have the relationships you want without going through the process. Every success you've ever had was a result of going through *The 5 Levels* (even though you may not have been aware of it).

As you grow as a person, you *automatically* go through this process. Now you'll be aware of what level you are in at each stage of change.

4 Benefits of The 5 Levels...

1. You discover you're not alone. Everyone goes through this process as they learn a new skill or set a new goal. You may feel that you are the only one struggling, but you'll learn that all phenomenally successful people struggle through this process on their journey.

2. You can see your progress. As you move through each level, you gain confidence as you see results. Confidence breeds inspiration and motivation.

3. You can see when you're stuck. You can recognize if you begin to shrink back. Although this can be painful, it is necessary to reveal your true values and *that's* progress.

4. You can share it with others. Family members, faith members, and those you work with can benefit from being aware of their level of "BEing"

What is a phenomenally successful person anyway?

Finally, what do I mean by *BEing* phenomenal?

The primary definition of **phe·nom·e·nal** is: Very remarkable; extraordinary

A phenomenally successful person is one that:

- Has a level of control over their habits and emotions.
- Is focused, inspired and knows what they want out of life.
- Is diligent and disciplined.
- Has a high score on the Wheel of Life (you'll learn about that in this book).

Are you ready to BEcome phenomenally successful?

Let's take the first step and find out who you *really* ARE...

Chapter 1

Phenomenal YOU

My training company is called *Phenomenal Products*. The reason it was named that is because when I started the company, we mostly sold information products (manuals, CDs and DVDs) rather than business training and coaching as we do today. Several years ago Bill Beckham, one of my early mentors, spoke at one of my conferences. As he opened his presentation, he said, "Howard's products *are* phenomenal, but I'm here to tell you that *you* are the phenomenal product. You're a special creation."

Zig Ziglar said that man was "designed for accomplishment, engineered for success and endowed with the seeds of greatness." He said, "You were *born to win*."

My guess is that you don't wake up every morning saying, "I am phenomenal." But you should. Why? Because you *were* created to BE phenomenal in all 7 areas of life: Physical, Mental and Spiritual, Family, Financial, Personal and Career.

In which of these areas were you created to be *unsuccessful?*

Of course, there will always be challenges and struggles in life. Many people have difficult circumstances; just surviving spells success. Success is doing the best with the hand you're dealt.

But let's examine each area for a moment...

1. Physical: Were you created to be unhealthy or healthy?

2. Mental: Were you created to be stressed or to have peace?

3. Spiritual: Were you created to be without a strong relationship with God or to know Him?

4. Family: Were you created to have relationship problems or to have harmony in your home and to be at peace with others as much as it depends on you?

5. Financial: Were you created to be broke and in debt or to prosper?

6. Personal: Were you created to have a sad life or to be joyful?

7. Career: Were you created to be unfulfilled in the work you do or to be fulfilled in the work you do?

If you believe that you were *created,* then you probably believe that you weren't created to be *unsuccessful, but* somehow in our society, many believe that they can't be successful in all seven areas of life.

Why is that?

Let's deal with being "created" first. Every human has 3 overarching, foundational beliefs:

1. What you believe about yourself. I call that your "youview."

2. What you believe about others. I call this your "worldview."

3. What you believe about God. "This is what I call your "Godview."

If you don't believe that God created you, your actions will reflect that. If you believe that God *does* exist, what do you believe about Him? If you believe that He's waiting to catch you doing something wrong, it will have a dramatic effect on your life.

If you believe that God created you for a special purpose, that your life is no accident, that He loves you - that you are a phenomenal product - and He has a phenomenal plan for your life, you'll have an entirely different experience in life. What do YOU believe about God? Can you see how that can have a dramatic impact on what you actually *do*?

What do you believe about others? Do you believe that other people are phenomenal creations of God? Do you believe others will help you? Do you believe that you can count on others? Do you believe that people can change? Do you believe that others can be trusted? Do you believe that people will give you a chance if you approach them the right way? Do you believe that if you help others get what they need, you'll get what you need? What does *your* worldview say?

These two beliefs contribute greatly to what we believe about ourselves - who we are, where we came from, and where we are going. These two beliefs also have a dramatic impact on what we believe about our future potential.

Did you notice that "believe" starts with "BE"? The goal of this book is to convince you that you were created to *be* phenomenal; therefore, you *are* phenomenal. In order to live that out and to *have* the phenomenal life you were created to have, you've got to BElieve it.

Special Notice: Please understand that I am not saying that humans don't do bad things and that everyone is "good." Are we sinners? Are we saints? Are we both? Are all people "bad" or "good"? Can we trust ourselves? My belief is that we are created by a good God, but born into a fallen, sinful world. Because of original sin, we were born separated from the very God that created us to be phenomenal. It doesn't seem right, but that's the way it is.

This was not God's intent. It was our free will. We inherited that. So, our journey in life is to come to know the ONE that created us to be phenomenal, so that we can really know who we are. Our beliefs about who we are, who God is, begins with what we think.

Proverbs 23:7 says, "A man is as he thinks."

A man at my church shared a story about his father who served in World War 2. They were captured by the Germans and put into a prison camp surrounded by barbed wire fence and armed guards. One morning, they woke up to find that the Germans were gone and the gates of the prison camp were wide open.

The immediate sense of joy and freedom soon turned to fear as they began to wonder if it was some kind of sick joke. If not, would the townspeople come after them with pitchforks? They just sat down and did nothing. They were free, but didn't act on that freedom for fear of the unknown. Later, the Americans arrived to rescue them. They were free all along but didn't know it.

What about you? Are you allowing fear, doubt and uncertainty to rule the day rather than focusing on the life you really want to live? My first book was called *7 Secrets of a Phenomenal L.I.F.E*; the acronym L.I.F.E. stands for Living In Freedom Every day. You see, there is no freedom living in fear and doubt. There is no freedom being locked up, mentally, emotionally, and financially and not knowing who you are (and Whose you are).

When I wrote this piece, I was staying with some dear friends at their home in Greece. My wife and I have been there before, and it was one of our best vacations; we were surrounded by sapphire blue water, exotic beaches and beautiful flora. My friends had some challenges and opportunities as it related to finances and business.

They came into the week with many obstacles, fears and challenges. I encouraged some brainstorming on the beach every day. After a couple of days of THINKING about solutions, we came up with a number of possibilities that would help them overcome their challenges.

They were locked up emotionally and couldn't see the potential. Since that time, they have exercised one of the options and all is well.

In order to get free from the stress of discouragement and fear, they had to allow themselves to *think* of possible solutions. When you change your thinking you change your beliefs. When you change your beliefs, you change your expectations.

In working with many small business owners, I often observe that they can't "see" see the possibilities. Time after time, they come to me feeling stuck. Recently, a man that owns four bowling centers came to me for a full day of consulting. He came in feeling limited, stuck, and without many options. He left with more opportunities and possibilities than he ever thought possible. Why? Because we took time to THINK about the possibilities without limitations.

Who do you THINK you are?

What do you THINK you can do?

Where do you THINK you can go?

The first thing to think about is your phenomenal dream. Why? Because your dreams fuel your life.

Are you ready? Let's dream a little.

Chapter 2

Your Phenomenal Dream

I'm a dreamer. Outside of the Grace of Almighty God and my phenomenal wife, Denise, I live a phenomenal life because I spend a lot of time THINKING and DREAMING - I call it "Intentional Dreaming." I've learned that if I don't spend time working ON my life instead of just living IN it, I won't get to where I want to go.

Since you have this book, you probably already know that I grew up on welfare in Alabama. I arrived in Houston, Texas, at 18 years old with 25 cents in my pocket. I became a waiter and started my first business out of the trunk of my car with $3,000.00 in wedding money. I wasn't good with money. I didn't know anything about running a business and I made many mistakes - most of them more than once.

I have to admit that my wife has always been good with money; she has gotten me out of financial messes that I got us into plenty of times. So, I had somewhat of an advantage even when I put us in credit card debt and made poor financial decisions. We weren't destitute. We have maintained a great lifestyle along the way even when times were tough in the businesses.

However, the key to moving from survival to stability and from stability to success and success to significance is being intentional. We have to intentionally focus on becoming a better person or it won't happen. Success doesn't happen by accident. It happens by *design*.

It all starts with the phenomenal DREAM.

Do You Have a Phenomenal Dream?

In his book, *Put Your Dream to the Test*, John Maxwell says that "a dream is an inspiring picture of the future that energizes your mind, will, and emotion, causing you to do everything you can to achieve it."

Without an inspiring picture, your mind, will and emotion won't be energized and you won't be empowered to do everything you can to achieve it, which means you won't take ACTION, which is the key to results.

Your Dreams Fuel Your Life

You see, without a compelling *why* - without a compelling vision - without a big *reason* to do something, you won't do the hard work that may be required to reach your goals. So many people want to be in a different place, but they won't allow themselves to see themselves in a different place. They won't allow themselves to dream, therefore, they won't do anything about their circumstances.

This book is about helping you know that you *can* reach your dreams. You *can* have phenomenal relationships with people. You *can* have a phenomenal relationship with God. You *can* be prosperous. You *can* be healthier. You *can* learn the things you need to learn to get to the next level, personally and professionally. You *can* change the world around you.

But if you don't have an inspiring PICTURE in your MIND, you won't get there. So, how do you get the picture? How do you dream? What if you don't have a dream?

Let's find out...

Intentional Dreaming means taking time to get in a creative, relaxed, inspirational environment to THINK, pray and dream. For me, it's the beach. To finish my second book, *The 5 Secrets of a Phenomenal Business*, I spent four days on The Great Barrier Reef. I was in Australia doing small business training for the Ziglar Corporation and The Great Barrier Reef was on my "bucket list." So I tacked on a few days there, knowing it would be an inspirational place to write, and it was.

There I followed my normal intentional dreaming routine: I get up early and write for a couple of hours (like I'm doing right now). Then I go out to the beach. After a swim, I sit down with a spiral notebook and begin to dream. There are no limitations; you simply allow your mind to drift. This is called "free association." Your mind begins with an idea and that idea leads to another idea and your mind associates one thought to the next.

When your mind is free to associate, your subconscious mind begins working on the problem or idea for you. This is the reason solutions come to you in the shower or when you wake up. Your mind has been free to drift and your subconscious mind is working out solutions.

Simply visualize your life with no limitations. Zig Ziglar called this a Dream List. Write down everything you want to BE, DO, or HAVE. Don't allow any negative thinking. Don't worry about not having enough money or that it is too big of a dream. Let it flow!

Here's an example... 15 years ago, I found my dream property - a gated community with only 14 home-sites right next to my favorite beach in the Destin area, 3 1/2 miles of unspoiled State Park beach. I've never seen more than a handful of people on that beach. The sand is sugar white with huge, magnificent dunes. The water is emerald green and crystal clear. It's truly paradise.

That beach is where I go to dream. For some strange reason, there's one specific spot on the beach where I seem to get the most "energy." When I discovered it in 1997, a single lot was $300K. At that time, we were just building our dream home in Houston and I had just launched Phenomenal Products. It felt like it was too much of a stretch. Over the next few years, the lots began to disappear and the prices began to soar. Before long, there was only ONE lot left! The homes were $3.5M minimum, which was way out of our range at the time.

My goal was to acquire the very last lot and to hold it until I was ready to build our next dream home. Unfortunately, by this time, the lot itself had gone up to $1.4M. Over a million dollars for a pile of sand! Yet I still dreamed and planned how I could acquire it. My thoughts were recorded in my journal. I was THINKING of ideas that would help me raise enough money for that lot.

I thought about it EVERY DAY.

I asked myself if investing that much money in a lot was too much and wondered if it would be "ungodly" to spend that much on a piece of land. I had many mixed feelings. After a while, I determined that if I was willing to work hard, continued to tithe and support the work of ministry, and continued to make a difference in other's lives it was okay. As long as it did not take from anyone else, I felt comfortable pursuing it.

But I still didn't have ideas big enough to acquire it. Looking back, that's not true. I just didn't THINK big enough. One of the "blessings" of the economic conditions from 2008 to 2011 (for me) was that the property values plummeted. The lot dropped to $633K, then to $533K. We became very serious about grabbing the very *last* lot in Stallworth.

I put in an offer for $410K. They countered at $490K, which I accepted. However, I only had three days to secure a letter of credit. We could have paid cash, but all of our investments were in 401k plans, annuities, and other assets that would cost huge penalties in order to cash out. This wasn't a problem, since our credit was really good and this property had been on the market for so long.

My Houston bankers didn't do Florida property, especially land, so I went to a Destin bank. The very first bank I went to assured me that financing the lot for me was not a problem; however, they were being bought out by another bank and all loan officers were in Atlanta for a meeting. "Not to worry," she assured me. Two weeks later, the real estate agent representing the property called to inform me that he had a cash buyer and that he had to take the other man's offer.

My dream property was gone.

I was stunned.

To add insult to injury, the letter of credit came from the banker the very next morning. I quickly forwarded it to the agent and pleaded that he deny the cash buyer and to accept my offer since I was first.

"It's too late," he said.

I was pretty bummed out that day. Did I miss it? Was it against God's permission? Was I totally off base? Over the years, I somehow thought I was "supposed" to have this property - I know that's weird, but that's how I felt.

After licking my wounds for a while, two amazing things happened. First, I've trained myself to be grateful for what I have. So, I began thanking God for the blessed life I have. I cannot complain and I had an overwhelming sense of gratitude.

To quote Zig a couple more times… "Of all the attitudes one can acquire, the attitude of gratitude is by far the most important and life changing." He also said, "Failure is an event, not a person." And finally, he said, "It's not what you GET by accomplishing your goals, it's what you BECOME."

IMPORTANT LESSON: Be content with what you have, but never be satisfied with your personal growth. Always be grateful for what you have, but always strive to BEcome a better person every day. Remember, it's not about the house and not about the stuff. It's about stretching your faith and your imagination to give you the experiences you need to help others.

It's about BEcoming.

When it comes to goals, sometimes you win by reaching the goal and other times you learn a valuable lesson (to quote another John Maxwell book title). You reached a goal of BEcoming a better person.

In the midst of this gratitude session, something amazing happened.

I had a thought...

"Wait, it's NOT OVER!"

Real estate deals go bad all the time. From the little experience owning a few properties and knowing many real estate investors, I knew the deal could go "south" even if it was cash.

Then, something even more amazing happened. I began to remember that I was "supposed" to have this property. It was mine! That was *my* dream. The other guy was a real estate developer. He wanted the property just for the money. I'm sure he has dreams like everyone else, but his goal was a lucrative real estate deal. My dream is to LIVE there with my phenomenal wife, to walk and pray on that beach, to THINK about how I can impact more lives and to DREAM about how I can do as much good during my one-time stop on this planet!

I'm risking being a little arrogant here; please stay with me.

Although I am GRATEFUL for what I have today, I am NOT going to let my dream slip away because of circumstances. God hasn't shut it down yet. A little circumstance called competition has gotten in the way. Am I just going to stand by and let someone take my dream away?

NO WAY!

So, I contacted the real estate agent (who is certain that I'm crazy at this point - I've called him just about every year for the last decade prior to this encounter). "Listen. I know this other guy supposedly has cash. But real estate deals go south all the time," I said, "I want to have my contract in play so that when this thing doesn't work out with him, we can move forward with our deal." At this point, I've gone from "if" the other deal doesn't work out to "when" it doesn't work out! He responded, "Well, this guy has cash and buys a lot of properties... I'm sure there won't be a problem..."I insisted, "I know you probably think I'm crazy, but I've got a feeling he isn't going to come through... how many days does he have?" "Seven," he responded. "Okay, will you let me know the minute this deal doesn't work out with him? And please put my contract in play as the first back up so I don't lose this opportunity again. You know I've been working on this a long time." I pressed. "Okay, I can do that, but I think it's a waste of time," he replied.

Every day after that I checked in with him by e-mail, text or a phone call, and made sure that I dropped a seed of doubt (sounds bad doesn't it?) each and every time. I would say something like, "Just let me know when it doesn't work out. I'm ready!"

Now he *knows* I'm crazy!

Seven days come and go. "So what's the verdict?" I texted. "The owner gave him three more days," he replied. "Hmmm... what's the problem?" I asked. "He's requesting the homeowners association move a boundary on the property." That statement gave me more confidence than ever because I knew one thing... That AIN'T gonna happen! "Okay, I'll talk to you tomorrow." (I'm sure that made his day.)

Three days later I left him a voice mail. "Are you ready to do my deal? The other guy is out, right?" A text comes back. "I'm working on putting you in first and him in second." Two hours later, his assistant sent over the contract and we bought the property.

The lesson I learned was to be grateful, content and patient, but to never give up if it's something you truly believe in and if you're not 100% sure that God has shut the door. How would I have felt if I gave up and found out later that the deal with the "cash guy" went south and someone else got my dream property?

SPECIAL NOTE: Although I am calling this a dream, in reality, it was just a big goal. This is what Michael Gerber calls a "personal" dream. The "impersonal" dream is something that can change the world - something that will change lives. I have a few of those, too!

Sure, we plan to put a beautiful home there that will serve as a dreaming place, a place where our friends can come to think, to dream and to be ministered to, just like our current dream home in Houston.

I used this as an example because it's a dream to me and everyone can relate to pursuing a goal like this. But please understand that at any moment, I KNEW God wasn't at least allowing me to have it. If it wasn't His will or it would harm someone else in any way, I would be quick to abandon it.

The point of a dream is to stretch you. It's to stretch your imagination. It's to excite you – to energize you. Einstein said, "Imagination is more important than knowledge."

I grew because of this experience. Now, I *know* now that I can do more. I'm working on even bigger projects now. Every time you get to the top of a mountain in any area of life and you see God give you a huge breakthrough that everyone thought impossible, you see an even bigger mountain that you KNOW you can climb. This is not only true in material things, but also relationships, movements, and every other kind of accomplishment.

You can do more than you think you can, but when you intentionally *think*, you discover how much more you can do! Remember, Zig said, "It's not what you GET when you reach your goals, it's what you *BEcome*" (*emphasis added*).

James Allen (*As A Man Thinketh*) said, "Dream lofty dreams, and as you dream, so shall you become…The greatest achievement was at first and for a time a dream. The oak sleeps in the acorn; the bird waits in the egg…. Dreams are the seedlings of realities."

How to Dream

Many people I know don't have a clear dream. They know they aren't truly fulfilled where they are now, but they aren't really sure what they want. In this chapter, I will share a few exercises that will help you discover your dream.

Beach Thinking

Intentional Dreaming requires freedom of thought. You cannot effectively dream when you are dealing with day-to-day pressures. Get away from your business every 90 days to think, dream and plan. That's why I go to beautiful beaches- the beauty inspires me.

I'm a beach bum. I absolutely love to just lie in the sun with a notebook and let thoughts come to me. The creative environment with the water, sun, and palm trees energizes my mind, will, and emotion. The solution to a problem just appears out of nowhere - this doesn't happen when you're under stress. In fact, you usually make the WRONG decision when you're stressed.

Getting away every 90 days for the intentional reason of thinking about your life and your business gives tremendous returns. Business retreats are held in relaxed environments because a relaxed, creative environment (like the ocean or the mountains) allows your mind to "freely associate."

Sabbath Thinking

About eight years ago, I began taking a full day off every week to allow my mind and soul to rest and to do nothing related to business. Although the Sabbath isn't on Sunday, it was the day I picked. At the time, Sunday began like every other day. I spent time writing, planning and checking e-mails. Deep into my projects, I would be late for church and the church building is three doors down! After church, I went back to work!

One Sunday morning I got a word from the Lord, "Not your words, but My Word." I decided to take it seriously and eliminated anything related to work on Sundays. No e-mails, no reading business books or articles, no phone calls related to business. Nothing. Then, something amazing happened.

I began to get my best ideas on Sundays! But a rule I set for myself was to not write it down. If I did, I would get sucked back into planning mode again. Then it got even better. That year I got more done and made more money than ever. How is that possible when you take a seventh of the week OFF and get MORE done?

Here's the "secret." Throughout the week, your mind is storing all sorts of thought seed, but it never has the chance to sprout. As you allow your mind to freely associate ideas, solutions to problems appear and new ideas emerge.

I learned that when you intentionally think about something, your subconscious mind attempts to make it a reality even when you aren't consciously thinking about it. So I began to give myself verbal problems on Sundays! I put my dreams, opportunities and problems in my mind every week. And what do you know? I'm still getting amazing answers from my soul eight years later. I highly recommend it.

How to Find Your Dream

Your dream is to simply live the life that you were born to live. It's that simple. Whatever it is that you do for a "living" is just a vehicle to help you live out that purpose and calling God has given you.

Most people say they have a dream, but they can't really describe the "picture" of the dream. Some are very clear. Others don't have a dream at all; they don't know what they want out of life. My first suggestion is to simply assess where you are on the Wheel of Life (shared in a later chapter). The rating is from 1 to 10, one being poor and 10 being phenomenal.

How would you feel about your life if you were a "border-line-eleven" in every area of life? Pretty good huh? So, just start there. If you do that and only that, you will do more than most in this life and you could be satisfied with your life. If you score a perfect 10 on a scale of 1 to 10, you've done well. As you do the Wheel Of Life Exercise and intentionally think about your life, I hope you'll discover your purpose and calling.

The Difference Between Dreams and Goals

My friend Rudy Ruettiger (the real guy from the movie "Rudy") told me when I was with him that "a dream is a feeling." Rudy had a dream of playing football for Notre Dame. He was too small, not smart enough and he didn't have the money to go to Notre Dame. But he never gave up on his dream. After he accomplished that dream, he had another dream. To make a movie about his life. People told him he was crazy. The movie is one of the most watched movies in HISTORY!

Michael Gerber says "a dream is the impossible." In his book *Awakening the Entrepreneur Within*, Michael calls it the *impersonal* dream.

The impersonal dream is the one that changes the world. The impersonal dream is a specific way that you impact the world. An impersonal dream is what Martin Luther King had. An impersonal dream is what Mother Teresa had. An impersonal dream is what Billy Graham had, a dream that makes a difference in others lives. That's significance, not just success.

My impersonal DREAM is that every small business owner on the planet will Live In Freedom Everyday (L.I.F.E.) – they will live in sense of community with others so they can experience the support, encouragement, and accountability that comes with that. Is that ever going to happen before Jesus comes? No way!

But, you see, that dream fuels my life. That is what gets me up every day. With that impossible, impersonal dream, I will pursue my VISION of small business owners meeting in small groups in every major city in the world.

The vision is possible (even if the dream isn't). How do I accomplish that vision? Through our MISSION of creating a sense of community in every enterprise and every group. But why? My PURPOSE is that they might have L.I.F.E., and have life abundantly. That each one would be a perfect 10 on every spoke of the Wheel of Life and that they would be helping others do the same.

It all starts with the dream – the impossible, impersonal, inspiring DREAM! Your dreams fuel your life.

A goal is a step toward the dream. The dream cannot be measured, but the goal can. The dream is the destination. Goals are the mile-markers along the way. If I'm going to my favorite beach in Destin from Sugar Land, TX, where I currently live, there are mile markers along the way that show me my progress. Having made the trip many times, I know exactly how long it takes to get to each city in between.

Of course, that depends on weather and traffic. Isn't that a lot like life? You have a vision, but many obstacles come your way. This is why vision and dreams are so important. Strong vision endures heavy crosswinds. You must live your life with a vision, not on circumstances.

Your DREAM TEAM

Discovering your dream involves discovering your passion and gifts. You'll find these by building your "dream team." Your dream team includes people who care about your success. Your dream team should include your peers, your staff and, of course, your family members. I'm so grateful for the long list of people in my life that encouraged me, inspired me, challenged me and most of all, helped me discover WHO I AM!

Leadership expert Dave Anderson said, "If you have a dream and no team, you have to give up the dream or build up the team." I don't know about you, but I'm not giving up my dream! So, I decided to build a team.

When I first started building a team, I didn't know what I was doing. So, I had to learn from others.

I began to serve people I thought were doing significant work - associations in my industry and my spiritual mentors in my church community. They began to help me see and practice my gifts.

Every human has a gift and that gift is irrevocable, but it takes a loving community to discover it. So, you need to be a part of a team to help you find your gift and your passion. As you begin to exercise your gift, the passion will come and the dream will become apparent.

My company, Phenomenal Products, is a great example of this. As I became involved in education within my industry, people began to notice the gifts I have. The desire to help others was already there. Then late one night, on a dark stretch of Texas highway, the THOUGHT of Phenomenal Products was born. I was with one of my employees when we began dreaming about how to help small business owners. The THOUGHT SEED was planted. This began the most significant chapter in my life, and as far as I can see, revealed the calling to my life.

Having a loving community to help you find your calling is critical!

What if those around you don't believe in your dream? What if that's your spouse? What if your spouse doesn't have a dream? What if they have a dream, but it conflicts with yours? Many times we get married young and we don't have enough awareness about our gifts, talents and dreams, and two different visions develop.

I know how you feel. My wife and I have been through that; My wife has been my biggest supporter over the years, but the problem was that I'm a big dreamer and she is very practical. Now, I had big dreams even when I didn't have any means of reaching them. I was handling my finances in a way that almost stole my dream from me. The way I acted was contrary to my actual dream.

My wife Denise is just the opposite. Not only is she very practical, but also very good with finances. She could do anything she wanted to do, but her "dream" was simply to see our son through college, hopefully have some grandkids, and make a difference in others lives on a daily basis. Life is good!

But that wasn't enough for me. In fact, I got a big vision standing in our kitchen one day. The vision was so big that I had my eyes shut and my hands in the air as I described the vision to my wife. I began with, "Honey, I see us doing this and that..." and began to explain the lofty, far out dream in detail. I opened my eyes to make sure she was on track with me. She stood there with her hands on her hips, tapping her foot, and said, "I've got a vision too – of you clearing out the dishwasher so I can load it!"

In John Maxwell's book, *Thinking for a Change*, he shares 11 types of thinking. One of them is Reality Thinking - that is what my wife is good at. I found that my gift is Possibility Thinking and hers is Reality Thinking. Together, we make a phenomenal team. I didn't know it at the time, but I see it now.

If your spouse is not currently on the same page as you, then talk to your spouse about their dream. If they don't have a dream or don't know how to dream, the best thing to do is show them some results of your dream. My wife began to believe in me more when I had some results to show - that's not unreasonable.

Please Hear This!

Becoming a phenomenally successful person involves sacrificing for others needs. If your spouse isn't in agreement with something that will affect their life, then putting your dream on hold is the right thing to do. Even if your dream includes affecting many lives, you belong to your spouse and your priority is there.

When I first came to know the Lord, I went headlong into ministry. For a period of time as my wife and I grew apart, I was painfully reminded that my first ministry is to my wife. By making that commitment to her and being willing to put the dream of being part of that ministry on hold, my true calling was revealed and developed. Now Denise and I are on the same page and have the same dream. You have to put something in before you can get something out, as Zig liked to say about his old water pump.

The Vision Board

Remember John Maxwell's quote from earlier, "A dream is an inspiring picture of the future that energizes your mind, will and emotions, empowering you to do everything you can to achieve it." You must intentionally put that picture in your conscious mind. When you put inspiring pictures in your conscious mind, your subconscious mind causes you to begin doing "everything you can" to achieve it.

As I was building my first company, we experience many growth pains. Through the frustration, a simple vision board continued to inspire me to keep going (not to mention much prayer and trust in God). The vision board was a poster of the Seaside Post Office in Seaside, FL. A quaint little post office set in a Victorian style village. If you saw the movie *The Truman Show* with Jim Carrey, you would recognize it, as that was where the movie was filmed.

I had a different movie playing in my mind. My movie was riding my bicycle around the village of Seaside where that little post office is located. I had a little basket on the bike and life was good! The beach was nearby and the sun felt good on my shoulders in that carefree dream.

My dream was to live near there, and in 2007 I purchased a condo on the beach. By this time we were in another office and that vision board was hidden somewhere in a closet. As I was purchasing the condo, I realized it was a very short bike ride from the little post office in Seaside. Denise and I ride our bikes through Seaside almost every day when we are at the condo. And yes, I have a little basket on the bike!

I used the same method to keep myself focused on my dream of owning property at Stallworth. I always looked at pictures of that beach. Now I have a vision board of an *impersonal* dream (as Michael Gerber calls it)...

A few years ago, I attended Michael Gerber's *Dreaming Room*. Michael Gerber is widely held to be the world's #1 small business expert. During the event, you are challenged to identify your Dream, your Vision, your Mission and your Purpose. This is outlined in Michael's gifted book, *Awakening the Entrepreneur Within.*

The Dreaming Room gives you a "blank piece of paper and a beginner's mind." You are required to draw your dream on a large artist's pad and given a bundle of multi-colored sharpies.

As you begin to work on your Dream, your Vision, your Mission and your Purpose, pictures begin to emerge. The picture of my dream included small groups meeting worldwide to learn how to become more successful in life and business. This dream is happening now! Of course, my family was there with the hand of God and the setting at the beach.

Create Your Own Vision Board

Draw out your vision or cut out pictures of your goals and dreams and post them on a Dream Board or Vision Board and look at it every day. Imagine it being real. THINK about it EVERY DAY. **Your Perfect Day**

Another exercise I love is the "Perfect Day" exercise. In this exercise, think about your perfect day. Think about the lifestyle you want to live (or the one that you truly feel called to), a lifestyle that truly inspires you and leaves room for God to work in your life.

Where do you wake up in the morning?

Who are you with?

What do you do when you get up?

What do you do next?

What do you do at lunchtime?

In the afternoon? Evening?

Outline your entire day. You may have several perfect days - like a day at "work" or a free day. The beauty is that is up to you because there are no barriers.

For me, I wake up with my princess Denise in Stallworth (our home on the Dream Beach). After coffee, I read the Word of God, pray and invest about three hours writing - Denise is still sleeping at this point. When Denise gets up, we have breakfast and then I go out to the beach for a walk and a swim.

Next, Denise will probably go shopping, so I will spend some time working on projects that are going to help more people experience L.I.F.E. (Living In Freedom Every day). I may deliver a webinar or work on my next presentation.

I have lunch with Denise, and then back to the projects. In the afternoon, I'll have a couple of phone calls with clients or partners. Then, I'll get my exercise by riding my bike or playing basketball. It's back to the beach after that to think and swim.

On some days, I'll participate in my Phenomenal Youth Program (another dream of mine) which is an after school program for kids.

In the evening, we have dinner with friends, participate in a community group, or hang out and watch television.

If I'm traveling to speak, I have a specific routine for those days as well. Please understand that everything I do has an underlying purpose - to help others experience Live In Freedom Every day - to be a "borderline eleven" in all seven areas of life.

The idea is to have a clear picture of your preferred lifestyle. If you don't have a VISION for something different than what you have now, then you won't do the hard work to get there.

For example, every year I go on a private retreat with some friends and family members. This past year we decided on Grand Cayman Island as the location. In order to convince my brother (who is a diver) to do Cayman instead of Belize (where he wanted to go), I had to agree to get certified in scuba diving - something I had no desire to do.

I love the water, but didn't want to bother with all the training, the gear, etc. The course was pretty easy, but I felt like it was too much work and time for what you get out of it. After spending three half days in the water, I still didn't really like it that much. Don't get me wrong, it was beautiful down there, but I just didn't have a big desire to do it.

You see, when there's an inspiring picture or a burning desire, you'll endure all sorts of discomfort to get there. But if the "juice isn't worth the squeeze," to quote my business consultant friend Ellen Rohr, you won't do the hard work to get there. You must have that "inspiring" picture that will energize you to do what it takes.

Take some time to write out your perfect day. Remember, there are no barriers for now.

Now let's learn about *The 5 Levels* of becoming phenomenally successful.

Are you ready?

Chapter 3

The 5 Levels of Being Phenomenal

The goal of this book is to help you understand the natural process all humans go through as we learn to *become* the person we were created to be. You already have the *potential* to be the person you are called to be. You already have the calling. You must merely discover *what* your specific calling and purpose is. Every human is created for a specific purpose. It is no accident that you are on this planet for such a time as this.

Zig Ziglar said in his last book, *Born To Win,* that it is our responsibility to discover our purpose in life. That's a tall order! To begin that process, you must begin to understand more about yourself, God, and the world so that you might step into the role you are supposed to play on the stage of life.

To find your specific purpose in life, you must surround yourself with wise counselors that can speak into your life. Phenomenal Products was founded on Proverbs 15:22, which says, "*Without consultation, plans are frustrated, but with many counselors plans succeed.*" As you discover your gifts and passion, you'll discover your purpose in due time.

Living out your MISSION, VISION and PURPOSE is when you'll truly be fulfilled. It doesn't matter how much money or material possessions you have, you'll be truly fulfilled when you are doing what you are *called* to do.

You'll struggle until you have a vision for your life. In this book, I'll show you how to at least outline some life goals. *The 5 Levels* will help you accomplish those goals and once you find your dream – your purpose – and your calling, the levels will help you with that, too.

Important NOTE: *The 5 Levels* are meaningless outside of a goal. Otherwise, it's just a muse. Whether you are reaching for a goal, developing a new skill, or kicking a bad habit, *The 5 Levels* help you understand the process you are going through so you won't quit - at least not easily.

Level 1: Self-Awareness

You become *aware* of your thoughts, feelings and habits. You become *aware* of a new idea or a new skill you want to develop. You become *aware* that a change is needed.

One of the best ways to illustrate these levels is physical fitness. In my first book, *7 Secrets of a Phenomenal L.I.F.E*, I shared how I went from being overweight, lethargic, and severely unhealthy to being *phenomenally* fit. I was 215 pounds (I'm five-eight). I drank coffee for breakfast and had lunch at two in the afternoon. By the time I got home in the evening, I was famished. I ate everything in sight and I do mean *everything*!

I started with a bag of tortilla chips and salsa as I prepared dinner, which consisted of a humongous stack of barbequed pork chops, a mound of mashed potatoes and bread. Of course, you've got to have dessert. My personal favorite was French vanilla ice cream topped with bananas drizzled heavily with Hershey's chocolate syrup. Now, of course this doesn't get you through a few hours of television, so back to the chips and salsa and how about a pickle or two?

How *low* does your self-awareness have to be to not know what the problem is?! Jeff Foxworthy might have a description for someone who goes through that routine every day and can't figure out why they're lethargic- "You might be a redneck!" And I was. I was totally unaware that my eating habits were the cause of my feeling so bad. Of course, I didn't exercise, either.

Level 2: Willing To Change

People only change through desperation or inspiration. I was desperate. I've always wanted to be productive and positive. My eating habits were making it more difficult by the day. My wife recommended I see a nutritionist so I could learn how to eat healthier. I was convinced that I would probably die young of an instant, massive heart attack, which was strangely okay with me since I knew the Lord (not being a very good steward however!).

The nutritionist painted a bleak picture. She said it probably wouldn't happen that way. Instead, like many Americans, I would probably have a couple of chronic diseases, dependent upon high blood pressure medication and insulin injections. This news gave the extra dose of desperation I needed.

I became willing to change because I became *aware* of new information that motivated me to change. Willing to change is where most people get stuck. Many people never get beyond that point because they never get desperate enough or inspired enough.

Instead, we stay in our comfort zone that's killing us. Like the proverbial frog that slowly boils to death as the water temperature slowly rises, we survive the day. Then, one day we wake up and we're just about cooked! Depending on what you're trying to change, there's a great deal of fear behind it. The fear of losing what we have is too great to move past this level.

Level 3: Controlled Attention

Once my nutritionist got me over the last hurdle (whether I could drink coffee or not), she gave me an eating plan to follow along with enough vitamins to choke a horse. I began to control my attention toward eating the right things at the right time. I began to FOCUS on the new routine. It was very uncomfortable at first. I couldn't drink coffee until I had been up for an hour. It was hard to figure out how to eat the right things when I was traveling; I faced many obstacles.

However, I stayed focused and began to see results. I dropped 10 pounds almost immediately. Before long, I was down by 38 pounds! And I wasn't done yet! It was going to get even better!

Now I was inspired! How far can I go? How fit can I get? How many pounds can I lose?

After getting through the FEAR of Level 2, you move into the stage of Controlled Attention. You apply a great deal of focus and attention to the new skill, idea or habit. It's uncomfortable because you've never done it before and your body and emotions are screaming at you like a baby crying for a bottle because they've become so accustomed to the old you.

Level 4: Commitment

When you become committed to a new lifestyle, habit or routine, you become more persistent and consistent. You are now hitting stride and getting results. Your confidence increases because of that. Your confidence might even turn into inspiration, as it did for me. The trouble with desperation is that once your back in your comfort zone, you begin to relax. If you start getting results and the confidence builds, it can turn to *inspiration*, which can carry you for awhile until you become committed to the new lifestyle.

For me, I got so encouraged by the results that I was getting and my energy levels were so high that I decided to start exercising. I began playing basketball every week and hired a personal trainer to work out with three times a week.

In less than a year, I had lost 50 pounds! I was lean and fit. I was super strong. There wasn't an ounce of fat to be seen. I couldn't believe it. I was so grateful, inspired and felt incredible. I had so much energy that I could hardly contain myself.

This was now a lifestyle. I BEcame committed. Commitment is a good place to be because it takes a lot more than just inclement weather to get you off course. It takes a major storm. At this level, your habits are beginning to take and you have almost forgotten your old ways.

Almost.

Commitment is not the end. It's just the level you must get to in order to enter Level 5...

Level 5: Character

Level 5 is when you have truly *become* the person you want to be. Level 5 is when your habits and values have changed. Your life and destiny are determined by your values. You do what you value and you value what you do. Therefore, your habits control you. The character level is where you've successfully shed the old habit and replaced it with a new one.

How do you know you've reached this level? Only time will tell. You might think you're in the Character Level, but you've just been in the Commitment Level for a long time. In fact, after five years of being incredibly fit, something happened. The perfect storm was brewing. I got bored with my trainer and it seemed increasingly difficult to make the appointments that I was committed to. It got to where I whined and complained about the exercise routines. I wanted to do something that was easier and it didn't help that I had nothing in common with my trainer. She and I argued about religion, politics, and just about everything else.

I fired my trainer. I deceived myself into thinking that I would exercise on my own. This was the first part of the perfect storm. The second part was already in play. Instead of going to see my nutritionist to pick up my supplements, I had them shipped. The lack of interaction with my nutritionist robbed me of the "motivational speech" she gave me every time I picked up my supply.

The kicker was a simple, seemingly innocent act that had big consequences. I had committed to not having a coffee in the afternoon. Although it was hard to get through that short 3pm hump, doing so helped my overall energy level in the evening dramatically. The afternoon coffee gave me a kick for a couple of hours, but as the old song "Spinning Wheel" goes... "What goes up, must come down."

At this point, I had fired my fitness trainer, I wasn't interacting with my nutritionist, and I had begun drinking coffee in the afternoons. My weight started coming back and my legs got weak due to the lack of strength training. Because of that, I blew out my knee playing basketball and had to have surgery.

Now, I'm laid up not being able to exercise at all. What do you do when you're in that situation? You get lazy. You get off your good eating habits and begin eating things you shouldn't. The end result is that I gained 25 pounds back. Each year I have to take a health assessment for our health insurance. When I was working my program, the assessment rated me as "super healthy." After backsliding, it rated me as "average." I don't know about you, but I don't want to be average. I want to be PHENOMENAL!

The good news is that all wasn't lost. At this point, I still eat pretty healthy - mostly organic and lots of veggies and greens. I'm still down 25 pounds. I still eat breakfast and I exercise regularly. But it's a fight. The inspiration eventually wore off and I found my true values. My true internal values say it's more important to be *relatively* healthy and to get more work done. My internal values show that other things are more important than exercise.

The Character Level reveals who we truly are. We do what we value and we value what we do. My goal is to get back to the "super healthy" stage. So, I will continue to go through *The 5 Levels* until I get back to that point.

You Keep Each Level As You Move Up

Something interesting to note is that each of the levels stays with you as you move up. For example, self-awareness runs through all of the levels. Self-awareness is the key factor to all of the levels. At Willing To Change, you will stay aware of your thoughts, feelings and actions as you uncover the fears, the roadblocks, and the challenges that you are going through as you decide whether doing the hard work of Level 2 is worth it or not.

When you move to Level 3, your Self-Awareness and Willingness to Change must stay intact in order to stay Focused. In order to operate in Level 4, you must remain Aware, Willing to Change and Focused. Level 5 happens automatically when you stay in Commitment long enough.

WARNING!

As I learned through my physical fitness journey, we may think we are at Level 5, but we aren't. Don't relax at Level 5. Michael Jordan did not relax once he became a Level 5 basketball player! In fact, the reason he was so good was because he competed with himself. His goal every night was to outdo his past best performances. Stay Aware, Willing, Focused and Committed even when you think you are at Level 5.

The Most Phenomenal News of All

The best news is that you *can* change. It's difficult today because many of us didn't learn the basic disciplines as children as children once did. Modern conveniences allowed the media to think for us and caused us to be lazy thinkers, full of fear and doubt. Don't let that happen to you.

Remember who you are (and Whose you are). You are a phenomenal product created to do phenomenal things and to have a phenomenal life. You were born to win. You were designed for accomplishment, engineered for success, and endowed with the seeds of greatness.

You can do this!

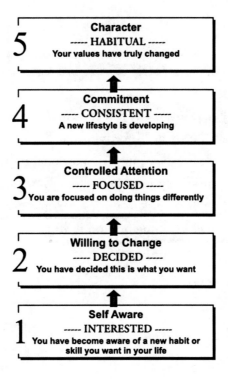

Chapter 4

Level 1: Self-Awareness

```
    ┌──────────────────────────────────────────┐
    │              Self Aware                    │
  1 │         ----- INTERESTED -----             │
    │   You have become aware of a new habit or  │
    │           skill you want in your life      │
    └──────────────────────────────────────────┘
```

How often do you think about what you're *thinking* about? How often do you ask yourself, "Why am I feeling what I'm feeling?" And when it comes to habits, too often, we put our emotional blinders on. We won't look at ourselves objectively because we may not like what we see. In order to change what you do, you must develop a curious, unemotional observation of your habits, thoughts and feelings.

Ask yourself these questions:

Why do I do the things I do?

Why do I feel the way I feel?

Why do I think what I think?

Then think about *what* you want.

Who do you want to *be*?

What do you want to *do*?

What do you want to *have*?

Self-Awareness must have a context in order to be valuable. Using this process without the context of your dreams and goals, is just a muse.

Perhaps an interesting exercise, but it doesn't have much value by changing who you are or what you have. In order to make this valuable, be clear on the habits you want to change and be clear on how you want to be different. Be clear on your goals.

Speaking of values, you do what you *value* and you *value* what you do. Be aware of what you do because what you do *is* what you value. I may say I value health above all, but if I eat ice cream every night before I go to bed, I don't really value health. The *truth* is that I want to eat ice cream more than I want to be healthy.

Mind, Will, and Emotion

Accept the TRUTH (the data - what is proven, not what you *want* to believe). Step outside of yourself and observe what you actually DO and don't do. Remember that there's a battle in your mind and *for* your mind. The mind says, "Don't eat ice cream. It'll make you fat." Emotion says, "I need it! I want it! I *deserve* it!"

Tom Ziglar says "what you feed your mind, determines your appetite."

Emotion cries out like a little baby and won't stop until your will settles it. Your WILL is revealed by what you actually DO, not what you want to do. Your will takes the input from mind and emotion and makes a decision.

Most of these emotions are driven by FEAR that may be hidden. Fear and emotion brings feelings that may or may not have anything to do with the truth. FEAR can produce anxiety, uncertainty, anger, discouragement and doubt. In fact, when you are successful, you may never *feel* successful. Some people never feel the satisfaction of success and significance. Your feelings don't represent the truth.

Self-Awareness allows you to FOCUS on the TRUTH and the TRUTH will set you free. You can't move forward in this journey toward new values until you face reality. Make a DECISION about what you really want. Make a DECISION about who you are. Don't let the FEAR of where you want to go keep you from getting there.

Watch your ACTIONS closely. Listen to the WORDS you use. Remember that you BElieve the things you say. Someone once said, "We lie loudest when we lie to ourselves." Zig Ziglar often said his motivational speeches helped him as much as anyone else. He also said the reason it's so important to be positive is because YOU are the one that spends the most time with you!

BE AWARE of your worldview. How do you value other people? BE AWARE of your view of God. How does that affect your actions? BE AWARE of what you think about yourself.

Step outside of yourself and...

Become AWARE of your actions and habits.

Become AWARE of your feelings.

Become AWARE of your thoughts.

Become AWARE of your words.

Become AWARE of your results.

Put all in CONTEXT of your goals and dreams

Facing reality is the first step. Become AWARE of your habits. Become AWARE of your attitude. Become AWARE of what you believe and why. Become AWARE of how you feel and what you are thinking about.

THINK about the limiting BELIEF systems which lead to your HABITS.

The Phenomenal Power of a TIME LOG

A great way to see what you value and what you don't is to keep a time log for 14 consecutive days. Simply write down everything you do each hour of the day from the time you get up to the time you go to bed. Do it in one hour increments. Jot down what you were doing the past hour.

Over 14 days your values will reveal themselves. You may see that you work on a lot of things you don't really want to work on. You may find that you get distracted easily and spend a lot of time on things that don't really matter that much. You might find that you are investing a lot of time doing "ten dollar an hour work" that you can delegate to someone else.

The *Ziglar Performance Planner* is a great tool for this. Zig logged his day in his planner every day. The planner has an area to give a plus or minus in the seven core areas of life. Zig assessed all seven areas of his life *every* day. The biggest benefit of the time log is that you will be AWARE of what you DO, which is the first step toward success.

The difference between phenomenally successful people and those who aren't is what they DO. Your HABITS determine what you do and what you don't. Your habits are determined by what you actually BELIEVE. What you believe is what you actually VALUE (whether we like it or not!).

What limiting beliefs do you have? What do you truly VALUE?

Self-awareness Tools

Here are some simple tools to assess where you are and to become a bit more aware of how you are hard-wired.

The Wheel of Life

A visual I have come to love is the Wheel of Life. I learned it from Ziglar and it is a powerful tool in personal

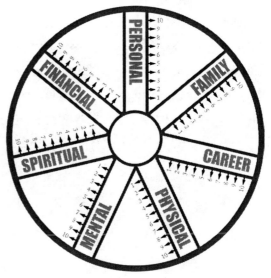

development. The reason I love it is because it not only gives you the PICTURE of what your life can look like, but it also gives you a way of assessing where you are right now.

We talk about GPS a lot in our business coaching. GPS helps you get from where you are to where you want to go, but the first thing it has to do is determine where you are.

On the Wheel of Life, you assess each of the seven core areas of life daily. Of course, the goal is 10 in each area.

The Seven Core Areas Explained

Personal - Your lifestyle, schedule and personal goals.

Family - Your relationship with family members (as it depends on you) - not their part, but yours.

Physical - Your ideal physical condition (as it depends on you) compared to where you are now.

Spiritual - Your relationship with God.

Financial - How successful you are in the area of money. It doesn't mean being rich, but it does mean not being in debt and being able to pay your obligations.

Mental - the knowledge you currently have compared to what you need to know to fulfill your mission and purpose in life.

Career - the role you fulfill in your company. If you are the owner, do you fill the position of doer, manager, or director, or is your business turnkey? If you work for someone else, are you fulfilled in the work you do? Are you doing what God has called you to do?

DISC: The 4 Behavior Styles

Another tool I really like is the DISC Profile. Everyone is "hardwired" just a little differently and understanding human behavior is key to becoming the person you are created to be. See? You were created to be a certain *type* of person. You were hardwired with unique abilities and a specific behavior style. Your behavior style determines what you are best at and determines how you communicate. Once you understand your behavior and communication style, you can understand why you do the things you do and why others do what they do.

There are many assessment programs on the market, but DISC is a very simple one that everyone can grasp easily and can be taught easily.

There are 4 Styles in DISC:

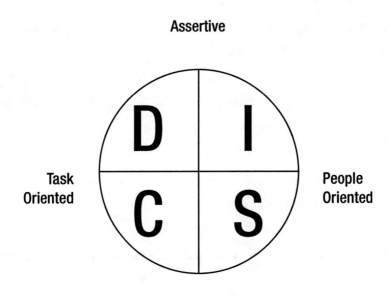

Two of the styles are "assertive" (D and I), meaning they are confident and outgoing. The other two are "reserved" (S and C), meaning they are slow to reveal emotion or opinions.

Two are "task" oriented (D and C), meaning if left to them, they would stay busy doing things rather than interacting with others. The other two are "people" oriented (I and S), which means if left to themselves, they will gravitate toward talking to people rather than working on a task.

This doesn't mean that a task oriented person isn't friendly and it doesn't mean that people oriented styles don't get work done. In fact, most people are a combination of two styles.

D = Dominance. The D Style is *direct, competitive* and *confident*. Their primary orientation is *results*.

I = Influencing. *The I Style is friendly, outgoing and emotional.* Their primary orientation is people.

S = Steadiness. The S Style is *sincere, loyal, and they are good listeners.* Their primary orientation is cooperation.

C = Competency. The C Style is *cautious, analytical, and by-the-book.* Their primary orientation is quality.

In order to determine your Behavior Style, please complete the following:

For each of the 10 word groups below, select the word that is MOST like you, LEAST like you, and IN BETWEEN. You are to assign 4 points to the word that is *most* like you, 3 points to the word that is *like* you, 2 points to the word that is *somewhat* like you, and 1 point to the word that is *least* like you. (There should be a 4, a 3, a 2, and a 1 on each line.

See the example.) Once you have completed this, follow the next set of instructions.

Example:

<u>3</u> Determined

<u>4</u> Convincing

<u>1</u> Predictable

<u>2</u> Cautious

1. ___Determined	___Convincing	___Predictable	___Cautious
2. ___Strong Willed	___Persuasive	___Easy-going	___Orderly
3.___Direct	___Expressive	___Kind	___Analytical
4. ___Bold	___Sociable	___Cooperative	___Precise
5.___Outspoken	___Animated	___Patient	___Logical
6. ___Decisive	___Talkative	___Loyal	___Controlled
7.___Daring	___Outgoing	___Agreeable	___Careful
8.___Restless	___Enthusiastic	___Considerate	___Thorough
9.___Competitive	___Inspiring	___Consistent	___Detailed
10.___Aggressive	___Playful	___Satisfied	___Accurate

Once you have assigned numbers to all 10 word groups, total the points for each column and write the total in the spaces provided below.

Totals: _____   _____   _____   _____

Styles: _____   _____   _____   _____

To discover what your behavior style is, see below. I didn't list it here because I don't want you to be swayed with your response.

The behavior style is also called your "communication style." We tend to communicate out of our BEhavior style. We are right back to the idea of BEing. We operate out of WHO we are. Awareness of *who* we really are, *where* we really are, and *how* we really communicate and behave is the first step to BEcoming a phenomenally successful person.

Remember, Zig said, "You are what you are and where you are because of what has gone into your mind. You can change what you are and where you are by changing of what goes into your mind."

You can't change how you are hardwired. That's a gift. You can't change your calling or your God-given purpose, but you *can* understand yourself better and you can develop yourself. Develop your gift and take measures to minimize the damage done by your weaknesses. Use this awareness to adapt to communication styles.

This is one of the simplest examples of an assessment. There are many behavior assessment programs that you can benefit from.

RESULTS: To find your DISC Behavior Style: Fill in the following letters in the spaces provided for "Styles" above. Your highest number indicates your behavior style.

	D	I	S	C
Styles:	_____	_____	_____	_____

Interested or Committed?

A man wearing orange pants stepped up onto a chair to give a 15-minute talk at a mastermind meeting I attended. Ron Eccles asked the audience, "Are you *interested* in success or *committed* to success?" For the next few minutes, he pounded on the difference. This is just the beginning. Perhaps you're interested in having a new habit or skill. You have four more levels to go.

Chapter 5

Level 2: Willing To Change

> 2 | **Willing to Change**
> ----- DECIDED -----
> **You have decided this is what you want**

Nobody likes change unless they created it. One of my early mentors often said, "Change is inevitable. Growth is optional." A couple of months ago, I had the pleasure to help launch the very first Zig Ziglar Legacy Training. It so happened that Dan Cathy, CEO of Chick-fil-A, was filming a legacy training interview the same time we were doing the training. So, Tom and I decided to make it a part of the training and filmed it in front of our small audience.

One of the many wise words that came from Dan Cathy was, "The rate of internal change must be faster than the rate of external change." Just like in the business world, we must change internally as fast (or faster) than things are changing on the outside.

In *Who Moved My Cheese?* by Spencer Johnson, two little mice named *Hem* and *Haw* had to be willing to change when all of a sudden their cheese was moved. If they didn't change, they went hungry. If *you* aren't willing to change, *you* might go hungry! And you'll definitely miss out on the wonderful goals and dreams that are waiting for you.

Change can be scary. Many people, when faced with the reality of where they are - although it's not where they want to be - find it too scary to change. They would rather endure the known failures and pain than to face their fear of the unknown.

It reminds me of the story of the old farmer's hound dog. As the mailman delivered the mail to the old farmer's house, the farmer was sitting on his porch with his hound dog lying next to him. The hound dog was moaning and howling, obviously in pain. "What's the matter with your hound dog, mister?" the mailman asked. "I think he's lying on a nail," the farmer replied. "Well why don't he get up and move?" the mailman asked curiously. "I guess it don't hurt bad enough yet," said the old farmer.

Humans can be like that hound dog. We have a high threshold for pain. We won't get healthy until it's a crisis. We won't do anything about our finances until we are so deep in debt there's nowhere to turn. We won't do anything about our marriage until it breaks apart. We won't do anything about our business until it starts to fail.

One of the big reasons we don't change is due to FEAR.

FEAR of Rejection - what if others don't accept me or my ideas?

FEAR of Failure - what if I change and I fail?

FEAR of Success - what if I can't live up to the "success" I achieve?

FEAR of Loss - what if I lose more than I gain?

Failure is required for success, but Zig said, "Failure is an event, not a person. Today is a brand new day. Yesterday really did end last night!" The fact is that you will have some setbacks if you decide to change. The real question is *why* do you want to change? Do you have a compelling vision?

While in Greece this past summer, I had a vision of building a $100M organization. As soon as the thought came into mind, the old negative thinking wasn't there anymore. I didn't hear, "Who do you think you are?"

Instead, I thought, "Hmmmm... what would I have to *do* to build a $100M company?" Just prior to going to Greece, I was in London with several of Zig Ziglar's best friends that all had companies valued in the tens of millions. If they can do it, I can do it. I only needed three things - an idea, a plan, and action.

The next day, I sat down on a rock overlooking the brilliant sapphire water and began writing out an idea and a plan. It came very easily. The simple process I used that anyone can use was:

I can sell one million of something that costs $100 every year, I can sell 500,000 of something that costs $200.00, or I can have 500 units of businesses doing $200K per year. This simple process led me to something I already knew how to do.

It *can* be done; but here's the challenge. I had trouble getting through Level 2. The plan I put together didn't excite me. I didn't have the passion for this particular plan because I couldn't see the benefits clearly. I couldn't see how much it would make a difference in others lives. I knew it would, but I didn't *feel* it yet.

Not too long after the trip, I encountered the vision on three more occasions. I had every reason to believe that I was supposed to pursue it. Not for the money, but because of what I will become and what it will do for others.

By March I had taken some very small steps toward the vision, but I wasn't pursuing it with the gusto I normally do. I wondered why. As I continued to think about it, I thought it was because I didn't want to risk what I already have.

I have a great lifestyle. Time with my wife, time to travel, and my work is making a tremendous difference in the lives of business owners around the world. I feared that pursuing this vision might cause trouble that would keep me from impacting many people. I wasn't willing to change. The passion for this particular plan was missing.

Then I discovered the reason. It came during a meeting with John Maxwell.

I'm currently one of only 14 people in John Maxwell's private mentoring group. Through that process, I discovered the problem was in the plan, *not* the vision.

The *plan* didn't excite me.

As I began THINKING about this, I came to a very exciting discovery. I could realize the $100M by pursuing a dream I've had for YEARS!

My dream of establishing local small business groups around the world would not only help me reach my goal, but it was my dream! Why didn't I think of that first?

After THINKING about *why* I was stuck at Level 2, I found the solution. After getting the right plan (that was tied to my purpose and passion), I was excited about it.

I took massive action immediately. I'm already developing leaders for the local areas.

When you spend time THINKING, you get solutions.

Can you see how Level 2 works? Can you see how easily you can get stuck at this Level? I had to have a burning desire before I was willing to change.

What about you? Have you made a definite decision to move forward? If you haven't, it won't happen by accident. Success is the result of hard work, passion, persistency and consistency.

Have you ever heard the "definition of insanity"? "Doing the same thing, the same way, over and over, expecting a different result!" This quote is attributed to Albert Einstein, a mathematician. Math CANNOT lie!

You may have heard "If you DO what you've always done, you'll HAVE what you've always had." "It's not true," Ziglar friend Billy Cox says. "Things are changing so fast in the world, that if you DO the same thing you've always done, you'll get LESS than what you've always gotten!"

In order to change, you have to get sick and tired of being sick and tired or you have to get so inspired that things just cannot stay the same. There are only two reasons people make extraordinary change: Desperation or Inspiration.

Sometimes it's both. My health change I mentioned earlier is a great example of this. I got desperate enough to get really healthy. I was tired, lethargic and overweight. I was desperate enough to change. I went to see a certified nutritionist and began to lose weight rapidly. Then, I got so inspired that I hired a trainer that came 3 times a week. I got incredibly fit!

Think about the seven core areas of life. What can you get desperate about? What can you get inspired about? Rick Jones, one of the business coaches we have on our team, was with Dale Carnegie for 33 years. He says, "All growth happens outside the comfort zone."

You see, there are three Zones:

Success Zone

Comfort Zone

Failure Zone

The problem is that most people don't try to climb to the Success Zone. They try to not fall into the Failure Zone by staying "comfortable." If you play to not lose, you will lose. The only way to win is to play to win.

If you play to not lose, you won't win.

You'll have some failures and setbacks along the way, but they are temporary and many times your biggest failures will lead to your biggest victories. Don't worry. There are many people that have cut the trail before you. You can learn from their successes and failures.

Play to win.

If you operate out of FEAR, your emotions will lock up your mind. You won't be able to think clearly and you won't be able to think creatively.

In order to THINK and BE a Phenomenal Success, THINK about the seven core areas of life and ask yourself two questions:

1. Are there any areas of DESPERATION?

2. Can I get myself INSPIRED in any of these areas?

In my business-coaching program, we have a slogan that says "Inspiration To Implementation." The most successful business owners are those who are excited. They are inspired. They can see things others can't. They have vision. They have dreams and they KNOW they are possible. They know that no matter the circumstances, no matter what anyone else says, they CAN be a PHENOMENAL SUCCESS!

You must KNOW that. If you aren't willing to change, you might as well put this book down now. Don't waste your time.

CHANGE is REQUIRED for GROWTH!

You will still have fear; all humans have fear. It's moving forward in the midst of fear because you are FOCUSED on the TRUTH. The truth that what one man can do, another can do. What one woman can do, another can do.

You simply must THINK that you *can*, DECIDE that you *will* and take massive ACTION.

Think, Decide, and Act.

If you make a mistake, just be willing to change again. Years ago, Pepsi was taking market share from Coke. Coca-Cola decided to change their original formula. There was public outrage. Everyone wanted "their" Coke back! Not only was Coca-Cola willing to change in the first place, after the public outcry they were also willing to change again after 77 days.

The original formula became Coke Classic. This is a great example of taking action and failing with a phenomenal outcome. Nothing could have solidified their uniqueness better than the public response that took place. Failure can bring you more success than you ever thought possible.

Stay focused on your VISION! Make a DECISION to change. Remember, when you change your thinking, you change your beliefs. When you change your beliefs, you change your expectations. When you change your expectations, you change your attitude. When you change your attitude, you change your behavior. When you change your behavior, you change your performance. When you change your performance, you change your life.

Have you THOUGHT about some areas you want to change in your life? Have you made a DEFINITE DECISION?

If not, you can't move onto Level 3. If you're truly willing to change and you've made a definite decision, let's move to Level 3: Controlled Attention.

Chapter 6

Level 3: Controlled Attention

```
   Controlled Attention
3      ----- FOCUSED -----
   You are focused on doing things differently
```

A few years ago, one of my friends introduced me to NASA astronaut Dr. David Wolf, the head of the spacewalk program there. He trains astronauts to work on the space station. He has been on four shuttle missions and is a brilliant man. My friend was writing a book about "success" words and asked Dr. Wolf what the most important word for success would be to him.

After thinking about it for a moment, he said, "Perspicacious."

My friend and I looked at each other thinking the same thing... "I have NO idea what that word means!" It means to have "acute mental vision or discernment." It has to do with staying focused in the midst of many distractions. Imagine all that could go wrong while spacewalking. The movie *Gravity* with Sandra Bullock and George Clooney depicted the worst case scenario. Perhaps not very realistic, but you get the picture.

Level 3 of *BEing* phenomenally successful is called "Controlled Attention." Controlled attention is the capacity to choose what you pay attention to and what you ignore. It is your ability to concentrate.

Transforming a new idea into a habit requires the *power of focus*. It is at this level where you'll be tried the most. At this point, you'll be tested to see whether you have truly made the decision to change or not, which will be revealed at this level.

Many people attempt this level without realizing how difficult it will be to see the new idea or habit through. We have a moment of inspiration and dive in before considering what is required to implement the new idea. This is where your comfort zone is really challenged.

You may have experienced this illustration before: Stretch your arms out wide. Now, bring your hands in to a clap. Cross your thumbs. If your right thumb is over your left thumb, then change will come very natural for you. If your left thumb is over your right thumb, you don't have a chance! JUST KIDDING!!! There's no truth to that, but here's the REAL exercise:

If your right thumb was over your left, reverse it. Put your left thumb over your right. If your left thumb was originally over your right, reverse it. Feels weird doesn't it? This feels *natural* to others! The only reason it feels uncomfortable is not because it's wrong; it's because you have a HABIT of doing it the other way!

While in Cambridge, one of my coaching clients, a dental implant specialist, drove us around. Although he has lived in England for 15 years, it still feels weird to him to drive on the left side of the road. I have to tell you that he got us to every destination safely and easily! You see? Even though it runs against his lifetime of conditioning, he can still be a "successful" driver.

As you move through this time of Controlled Attention - having a tremendous focus on what you have to *do* - you must keep your dream in mind. When you remember *why* you are doing what you are doing, you'll have more inspiration and commitment to stay on course.

"All Growth Happens Outside the Comfort Zone" – Rick Jones

Rick Jones, who is one of our coaches, was with Dale Carnegie for 33 years and owned the Houston franchise for 20 years, he is well-known in our coaching community for saying, "All growth happens outside the comfort zone."

Controlled attention is much like exercising willpower. It's kind of like breaking an addiction. Addicts continue to go back to the behavior they despise. Habits that are connected to strong emotional bonds can easily become addictions. That's why it is so important to understand WHO you were created to BE, to commit to that, and to stay AWARE of your daily thoughts, feelings and habits.

It is also vital to have a burning desire that drives you. You will NOT work through this level if you aren't going for something that is truly meaningful. If it is just a "wish," it won't happen. If the passion isn't there – if the burning desire isn't there - you won't have the determination to see it through.

A BIG Question

Do you have the DESIRE to have a better life? Do you have the desire for success? Do you have the desire to make a difference in other lives? It all starts with a dream. If you don't have a specific dream beyond your "Wheel of Life," then start there. How would you feel if you were a "borderline 11" on each spoke? Excited?

Perhaps once you get some success, you'll begin to pursue significance. I have a plaque in my office that says, "Success is making a difference in the lives of others. Happiness is watching them grow because of it." The reason I wrote this book is because it makes me happy to see people grow. What gets me up in the morning is to see people reach their goals.

The 4 Stages of Competence

Unconscious Incompetence - We are UNAWARE of our incompetence.

Conscious Incompetence - We become AWARE of our incompetence.

Conscious Competence - We are AWARE of our competence.

Unconscious Competence - We become UNAWARE of our competence.

Several years ago, I began playing basketball with some friends; I was terrible. Playing sports is a great lesson in awareness. I didn't realize many of the things that I was doing wrong. For example, my fellow players pointed out that I had my head down when I dribbled the ball; therefore I wasn't aware (there's that word again) of where my teammates were on the court and what the defense was doing. It never occurred to me that you have to dribble the ball with your head up so that you can look around to see what's happening.

I never played basketball at school like my fellow players. They were so gracious to me and allowed me to continue to play even though I constantly made mistakes. As I began to realize how woefully incompetent I was, I became willing to change and it took a tremendous amount of focus to get better. I was willing to do the work because I had a great desire to play and to be better.

As I became "consciously incompetent," I began to focus my attention on the various skills I needed to develop. I began to get better and moved into "conscious competence" in a few areas (like shooting from the outside) by *practicing* heavily and often. Now that I have practiced the skill many years, there are days where it seems that things happen almost automatically.

Michael Jordan probably operated in Unconscious Competence much of the time. It took many years of practice AND experience to get there. I heard Meadowlark Lemon (from the Harlem Globetrotters) speak once and he said that the reason Michael was so good was because he spent time in the gym EVERY DAY practicing the fundamentals like layups. Layups! Michael Jordan practiced layups? Yep.

You have to *practice* the simple steps to recognize your negative self-talk. You've got to *practice* reminding yourself who you are every day. You've got to practice by looking at your dreams and goals every day. It doesn't happen by accident and it doesn't come easily.

The payoff is that as you begin to reach small goals (like layups), you'll then begin to hit the bigger goals like the jump shot and the three-pointers. I've won a number of basketball games as a result of learning and practicing. I'm sure you have areas in your life where you've done the same. I want to tell you that the process of reaching goals and changing your behavior is exactly the same.

The NBA Finals or the Super Bowl are not won on game day. That DREAM is won by achieving a long string of small goals along the way. The late great basketball coach John Wooden said, "The game is won or lost in *practice.*" Zig Ziglar said, "You were born to win, but to be the winner you were born to be, you have to plan to win and *prepare* to win."

BElieving that you were born to win is the start. It tells you that you CAN. Regular planning helps you to establish the vision in your mind that inspires you. Preparing is practicing. It's training. If you train as hard as you fight, you'll win more often.

As you move through this time of Controlled Attention - having a tremendous focus on what you have to DO - keep your dream in mind. When you remember *why* you are doing what you are doing, you'll have more inspiration and commitment to stay on course.

The Power of the Time Capsule

One of the tools that will help you stay focused is a planner. I use the Ziglar Performance Planner, of course. The planner is used to record your dreams and goals and to stay focused on taking the action that will get you to your goal. It's very easy to get distracted.

To stay focused, I stay committed to what I call The Daily Time Capsule. Many years ago, I began to take an hour a day to work on my projects, early in the morning when everyone else was asleep. During this "capsule" of time, I didn't take phone calls. I didn't do chores around the house or get distracted with entertainment. This is a time to work ON the business. The only person that could find me is my wife.

I began this procedure when I ran my first business; I had to be at the shop by 7:30am, which meant I had to be up at 5am. I'm an early riser, so that was okay with me. I had big dreams, so I had the inspiration to do what needed to be done. Don't underestimate the value in being inspired about your vision. If you aren't inspired, you won't implement! It's that simple. Keep dreaming until you get the vision that inspires you.

When I started Phenomenal Products, the goal was to write a few manuals, which were to be my first products. In addition to working on the projects for my business (working on policies and procedures), I wanted to create these manuals. So, for about six weeks I got up at 4am instead of 5.

WARNING: When you get really inspired and excited, you might have trouble sleeping! Sometimes I woke up at 3am and couldn't go back to sleep. So I got up and began writing. I finished those manuals in 6 weeks and launched Phenomenal Products.

I still use the procedure today. My routine, after I wake up, is to get coffee, read a chapter from the Word of God, pray, and then write for an hour or two. Then I begin working on my projects. This happens six days a week, no matter what. The only exception is if I'm training that day; I'll do a short Time Capsule and may not do any significant writing. I'll spend an hour or so to keep my projects moving forward. It involves delegating by e-mail, building PowerPoints, writing scripts, ads, policies and procedures, communicating with partners or what have you.

In the chapter on goals, I'll share how my time capsule works.

But for now, let's focus on the next level. If you stay focused long enough, you'll eventually reach Level 4: Commitment.

Chapter 7

Level 4: Commitment

4	**Commitment** ----- CONSISTENT ----- **A new lifestyle is developing**

The commitment level is the level of consistency. At this level, habits are beginning to form. Things are happening a little more easily - you're developing a rhythm. It no longer feels like the wrong thumb was crossed. Your new skill is coming along. You're feeling more comfortable with the new routine. You've had some wins. You've had some base hits and maybe a few home runs. It's kind of like hitting that perfect golf shot. Now you're hooked!

At this level, you're also gaining confidence. Confidence breeds motivation and inspiration. John Maxwell says, "Commitment is being bound emotionally or intellectually to a course of action… commitment is dedication."

You probably remember how the chicken and the pig demonstrated commitment at the breakfast table. The chicken (who provided the eggs) was involved, but the pig (who provided the bacon) was committed!

I don't want to spend time talking about what commitment is because we can clearly see when we're committed to something or not. Instead, I want you to be intentional about moving into the commitment level.

You'll become committed when you truly BElieve in what you are doing. I can tell you to be committed, but if the drive isn't there, it's because your desire isn't where it needs to be, you don't have the discipline you need, or you don't have the support of a dream team.

When you're committed, you take action. You invest time developing your idea or skill because you VALUE it. Every level reveals your VALUES. This is what is so powerful about this process. Whatever level we find ourselves in helps us to evaluate where we are on the journey.

Let me take a moment to recap what we've covered so far:

1.   You BEcame AWARE of a new idea you wanted to pursue, a new skill you wanted to develop or a new goal you wanted to reach.

2.   You BEcame WILLING TO CHANGE because the desire won over the fear.

3.   You BEcame FOCUSED because you're convinced the time, money and energy invested will be worth it.

4.   You BEcame COMMITTED because you got some results from controlling your attention to it.

Zig Ziglar said, "Commitment helps you overcome obstacles." People who are committed expect to win; therefore, they plan and prepare to win.

BEing committed is a powerful thing, but you're still vulnerable. May 1st of 2005 was a significant day in my life. It was the day I made a DEFINITE DECISION to be healthy. I became painfully *aware* of my physical condition. I was willing to change and I did. I began to focus on eating right, began strength training three times a week, and played basketball every Sunday. I moved into the Commitment Level. It was now a lifestyle, or so I thought. After six years, I fell off the wagon.

What happened?

I stopped training. I was too busy. I had my assistant pick up my supplements from my nutritionist, so there was no interaction with her. I was no longer getting input from my trainer or my nutritionist.

To stay committed, we need support. We need a Dream Team. And we need one more than ever. Yes, we need our dream team to discover who we are in order to discover our gifts, our purpose, our strengths and weaknesses. We need our dream team to help us stay focused. We need our dream team most at the Commitment Level.

The reason is that we can easily fool ourselves. We fall into the trap that success came automatically. We forget how much we had to sacrifice to get here. Now it seems easy. We need our dream team to encourage us, to support us, and to help us stay accountable to do the things that got us this far.

We need dream team members in each area of our lives. I fired my trainer and didn't hire another one. I was "too busy" and I was bored. It wasn't fun anymore. I lied to myself by telling myself that I would do the work on my own. I didn't. My assistant was picking up my supplements from my nutritionist so that I missed out on that accountability. I was no longer getting the input from the two dream team members that helped me remain committed to phenomenal health. To stay committed, stay plugged into your support system – your dream team.

The Key to the 5 Levels is Support

Jim Rohn said, "You'll be the average of the five people you hang around." He said, "Who am I around? What are they doing to me? What have they got me reading? What have they got me saying? Where do they have me going? What do they have me thinking? And most important, what do they have me becoming? Then ask yourself the big question: Is that okay?" He also said, "You'll be changed most in life by the books you read (what you put into your mind) and the people you meet."

What will help you move through *The 5 Levels* more than anything is your dream team. We all need encouragement, support, and accountability. You need your dream team around you. Coaching and mentoring has made a bigger difference in my life than anything else.

It has taken me through *The 5 Levels* in all seven core areas of life.

My business-coaching program is unique because we do small group calls every week. Every member has the opportunity to be on a call every week with the same group of people and a facilitator that will help them stay focused, encouraged and accountable. The reason we do this is because everyone needs these three things. Everyone needs support. Everyone needs encouragement. Zig said, "Encouragement is the fuel people run on." We all need accountability.

We all need it and were created to need it. Proverbs says, "Bad company corrupts good morals." You may not have "bad" company, but you may not be keeping the kind of company you need to keep. People who will keep you accountable will encourage you and will support you - people who believe in you.

One of those people for me is Rick Jones. Rick was with Dale Carnegie for 33 years and owned the Houston franchise for over 20 years. My wife Denise, who sells radio advertising, called him and became friends with him. As it turns out, Rick is from my hometown, Mobile, AL. We became friends as well and I invited him to speak at my conferences once in a while. After selling his franchise a few years ago, he began searching for something meaningful to get involved in. Please understand that his financial needs were taken care of and his experience afforded him the luxury of doing just about anything he wanted to do.

He was looking into other franchises. I asked him to have lunch with me so that I could share with him what I was doing with Ziglar and how my coaching program impacted small business owners. He really loved what he saw and decided to join my team.

Rick has poured into my life personally and professionally. He taught me how to present better from the stage and how to be a better coach and trainer. He showed me my gifts and encouraged me that I could be as good as any of them out there. Rick mentored me, coached me and encouraged me every step of the way. It wasn't a job to him. Before he started, he said, "I want to spend some time with you first." Over a six-month period, he came to my events and we attended leadership conferences together. We went to see John Maxwell, Henry Blackaby and many others. We talked about life, leadership and our purpose in life. He told me that he had already made money and built a career. His new goal was to find a place where he could have a positive impact on people.

Before he chose us, he said, "Let me try it out for six months." So he began coaching our members using my systems. He refused to be paid for SIX MONTHS! I kept asking him, "When are you going to let me pay you?!"

After six months, he agreed that this was what he wanted to do. What I learned later not only encouraged me, but also floored me... I was facilitating a small group of our coaching members on John Maxwell's *Put Your Dream to the Test*. Rick was not in the room and one of our members who was coached by him said, "I once asked Rick what his dream was..." "What did he say?" I asked, "To help Howard be successful."

I still tear up when I think about that. To have a man with his wisdom and experience believe in me and pour his life into me and our community overwhelms me. Speaking of our community, the support, encouragement, and accountability I get from them is just amazing. Several of them have become some of my best friends. Our events are more like a family reunion than a seminar!

You should have one or more dream team members in each area of your life.

Here's what it looks like for me:

Physical: I now see my nutritionist every quarter. I have a new trainer and I'm killing it on basketball! I have a 22-foot outside shot that earned me the nickname "flame thrower." You had better cover me good on the outside!

Mental: The nature of what I do keeps me on my toes. Plus, I love to learn, write and think. The support, encouragement and accountability I get come from my business mentors - to stretch my thinking to the next level.

Spiritual: We have a small group that meets every other week. I have many people in my life that support and encourage me in that area. I meet with my various mentors from time to time to discuss life.

Family: I have many people around me that I have given permission to speak into my life. Years ago, Denise and I were really struggling with our relationship- two high D's colliding on a regular basis. My oldest brother and one of my mentors helped me through it. Without them, I don't know where I would be.

Career: The mentoring group I am in with John Maxwell kicked off the initial meeting with a dinner. Each of us had to go around the table and share the best advice we had ever received. Mine was "Get around people who have already done what you want to do." I could write a book on how Zig Ziglar, Michael Gerber, John Maxwell and many other coaches, consultants and mentors have helped my career. It's the key. Business is all about relationships.

In fact, I didn't want to write my first book. I had the (erroneous) idea that I was going to build a platform and have an instant best seller after I was well-known. Mark Ehrlich, one of my mentors who helped me find my true calling, sat me down in a Las Vegas hotel room and convinced me that I needed to get my story and message into a book. My first book helped me build my platform! Sometimes, we don't know what we don't know. And if you're anything like me, you think you know, but you don't!

Every successful professional has coaches, consultants and mentors.

Financial: I've always been good at making money. The problem is that I've always been good at spending it, too! When I was building my first business, I had two partners. Scott Zack handled the financial part of the business and was very conservative. He can manage money like I've never seen. He's a huge Dave Ramsey fan and hates debt and the poor guy had a partner like me!

I didn't care how much money we spent. If we needed something, I just went and bought it on credit. I used what I call the "Elvis Presley Accounting Method." Elvis would buy a stranger a Mercedes that cost 80 grand. Back at Graceland, his stepfather Vernon and his wife Priscilla were alarmed at the piles of bills coming in. Elvis' response was, "Don't worry. We'll just get another gig!" And he could. He would simply call "The Colonel" Tom Parker and do another million dollar show. When Elvis died, he was worth a mere $7.5M - much less than what he could have been worth.

I lived like that for a long time. By then, the debt piled up and life became about making the monthly payments. NOT very phenomenal! I became painfully AWARE of how my financial values were affecting me. Ellen Rohr, one of my consultants helped me get my business profitable and Scott Zack became one of my staff members after being my partner. Neither of them ever let up and eventually, my awareness turned to WILLING TO CHANGE. I began to CONTOL ATTENTION to my financial life.

Before long, I moved into the COMMITMENT level. Now we are phenomenally successful in the area of finances. We don't carry any credit card debt in our personal or business life and we give away a lot of money. The businesses are hugely profitable. I can promise you that if it hadn't been for people like Scott Zack and Ellen Rohr, I would have never truly committed to it.

Personal: When it comes to our personal lives, we need all sorts of people in order to make sure that we take some time for ourselves and that we have productive habits. I love the beach, so I always have a trip to the beach scheduled. It is my reward and my accountability piece. Part of this book was written while I was in the Cayman Islands with my "framily" (friends and family).

My mama, my aunt, my big brother, my wife and a few friends were there - 14 of us in all. I unplugged everything digital and had my staff post on Facebook and check my e-mail for me. I spent the first half of every day by myself reading and writing. In the afternoons, I went scuba diving with my brother and one of my phenomenal friends, Bruce DeLoatch. In the evening, we all had dinner together in the three story house.

It was great fun, but at the end of the trip, I realized that I didn't have as much fun as everyone else did. I felt a little empty compared to how they had bonded to one another. My mama and brother are always on me about "working so much" while on "vacation." This trip showed me that I probably ought to chill out a bit more and have a little more fun (Don't tell them I admitted that!).

We do a trip every year together, so I think next time, I'll not only unplug digitally, but also take a *real* vacation.

How to Stay Committed

You must discover your dream, your calling, your purpose, your big why or whatever you call it and keep it in front of you every day. Did you do a Vision Board? Did you write out your perfect day? Would you be inspired to be a Perfect 10 on the Wheel of Life? Keep the vision in front of you. Remember *why* you are doing what you are doing and stay plugged into your support team.

Stay plugged into your support system. It's too easy to think, "I've got it from here." Remember, we all need support, encouragement, and accountability.

Commitment is a phenomenal place to be, but it isn't the ultimate level. This is a good level, far beyond where most people get. At the commitment level, you are going to do the right thing most of the time, but if the perfect storm hits, you can still be blown off course because the new idea or skill isn't *part* of you yet.

"Victories attained by right thought can only be maintained by watchfulness. Many give way when success is assured and rapidly fall back into failure." – James Allen

It hasn't become part of the fabric of your being. Your goal is to *become* a different person than you are now. Your goal is to BE a different person today than you were yesterday. This happens by continually taking the ACTION you know you should take.

Once you stay at the Commitment level long enough, you'll move to Level 5. Level 5 is the ultimate level. Are you ready for it?

Chapter 8

Level 5: Character

```
    Character
5   ----- HABITUAL -----
    Your values have truly changed
```

Here's a riddle...

"Who Am I?"

I am your constant companion. I am your greatest helper or heaviest burden. I will push you onward or drag you down to failure.

I am completely at your command. I am easily managed – you must merely be firm with me.

I am the servant of all great individuals and alas, of all failures as well. Those who are great, I have made great. Those who are failures, I have made failures.

Show me exactly how you want something done and after a few lessons, I will do it automatically.

I am not a machine, though I work with all the precision of a machine, plus the intelligence of a human.

You may run me for profit or run me for ruin – it makes no difference to me. Take me, train me, be firm with me and I will place the world at your feet. Be easy with me and I will destroy you.

"Who Am I?"

I Am Habit.

Level 5 is when you have truly *become* the person you want to be. Level 5 is when your habits and values have truly changed. Your life and destiny are determined by your values. You *do* what you value and you *value* what you do.

Therefore, your habits control you. The character level is where you've successfully shed the old habit and replaced it with a new one. How do you know you've reached this level? Only time will tell.

As you continue to be aware, you continue to change, you continue to stay focused, and you stay committed. Eventually, habits will form. Your habits define you. I can say that I value health at the highest level, but if I have a habit of eating a quart of ice cream before bed every night, I have to admit what my true value is. Eating ice cream!

If you say you value honesty, but you find yourself bending the truth, you don't truly value honesty. If you say you're a good leader, but you yell and scream at your staff, you're deceiving yourself. Your reputation is what others think about you. Your character is who you actually are. When your reputation and your values match, you are living a life of integrity. John Maxwell often says, "True success is when those closest to you respect you the most." That's when you know you are living a life of integrity.

You may have good moral character, but you don't always make the right decision or do the right thing in every situation. Remember that developing yourself takes time. Correct your action. Remember the person you were created to BE and the person you are BEcoming. Remember that values change slowly and habits take time to develop. Developing the character we really want and living out the values we truly want to live requires new habits. Habits don't change overnight.

It has long been reported that it takes 21 days to change a habit, but recent studies reveal that it takes anywhere from 18 to 245 days, depending on the person and the habit.

Here's what John Maxwell has to say about Character in his training program on *The 15 Invaluable Laws of Growth:*

"Character growth determines the height of your personal growth. Think of character as climbing a ladder, getting you much higher than if you didn't have that ladder.

When you're better on the inside (character) than on the outside (reputation), over time you will become better, greater on the outside. When you are stronger and better on the inside than you are on the outside, *over time* a lot of good things are going to happen on the outside.

"But when you're better on the outside (reputation) than on the inside (character), over time you will become less on the outside."

So far, I've talked about having a vision for your life and the burning desire to BE a different person than you are today. Desire is the key ingredient.

In his book, *The 7 Habits of Highly Effective People*, Stephen Covey said, "For our purposes, we will define a habit as the intersection of knowledge, skill and desire. Knowledge is … *what we do* and the *why*. Skill is the *how to do*. And desire is the motivation, the *want to do*. In order to make something a habit in our lives, we have to have all three."

Once the desire is there, we can acquire the knowledge and skill of changing habits. In fact, as you begin to study this subject, you discover that success is a habit. Attitude is a habit. According the ground-breaking book, *The Power of Habit* (*Why We Do What We Do in Life and Business*), by Charles Duhigg, even willpower is a habit that can be developed. The point is that habits can change and values can change. You are now aware of the process that all humans go through as we attempt to change.

Here are a couple more important excerpts from the book:

"Habits never really disappear. They're encoded into the structures of our brain, and that's a huge advantage for us, because it would be awful if we had to relearn how to drive after every vacation. The problem is that your brain can't tell the difference between bad and good habits, and so if you have a bad one, it's always lurking there, waiting for the right cues and rewards."

"Habits are powerful, but delicate. They can emerge outside our consciousness, or can be deliberately designed. They often occur without our permission, but can be reshaped by fiddling with their parts. They shape our lives far more than we realize – they are so strong in fact, that they cause our brains to cling to them at the exclusion of all else, including common sense."

Once more from *As A Man Thinketh* by James Allen

"Men imagine that thought can be kept secret, but it cannot; it rapidly crystallizes into habit, and habit solidifies into circumstance.

"All that a man achieves and all that he fails to achieve is the direct result of his own thoughts."

How Values Change Most Effectively

I shared in the last chapter that in order to stay focused and committed, we need a dream team. Our dream team helps us stay aware of our actions, intentions, motives and values. Now, I want to submit the ultimate "secret" to changing our values and the secret to helping others change.

This secret came to me many ago as I noticed something about "church." On Sundays, a large group of people sat and listened to a sermon, but you really didn't notice any big changes in the members. But on Tuesday night, some of the members met at homes in small groups. At these informal groups, real ministry was happening. This one had a word, this one had a song, this one had a need, and so the group helped one another and supported one another. Real change took place.

Then I began learning about the small group movement in churches. I had the pleasure to be mentored by two pioneers of this movement, Dr. Ralph Neighbour, Jr., and Bill Beckham. From them I learned the secret of the small group. I learned the secret of true values change. I learned that values change most in a *community* environment.

Community is a word that has many meanings for many people. We often use it to refer to our neighborhood or our local area. We sometimes refer to groups of people as a community, such as the "Asian Community." We also talk about the "global community" and even the "virtual community" when it comes to the Internet. But my definition of community goes much deeper than just a neighborhood or a group of people...

True community is the sense of belonging that all humans hunger for.

We all have a longing for belonging. We all have the need to be connected to other people, a deep desire to be a part of something meaningful, something that makes a difference. The longing for community is the reason people join clubs. It also happens to be the reason people join gangs.

Our own family is the first community we all belong to, but the family community that existed in the pre-modern world has all but vanished. The idea of being deeply involved in each other's lives, enjoying each other's successes and enduring each other's failures seems to have disappeared. Unfortunately, losing this sense of family community has spilled over into every aspect of our lives, including our business lives. As a result, our organizations today mirror—and foster—the separateness we all feel.

And yet, as we pursue our individual agendas, deep down we all long to experience community as we once did. It's not only those who remember feeling a sense of community in the past who yearn for it. All of us do. We are created to BElong.

Social media has given a sense to some that they belong to a community, but the truth is that these are only virtual communities. A virtual community is an oxymoron. True community requires the human touch.

As a result, many young people have never felt true community. They've never felt the love and encouragement that true community can bring - they long for it. They may not even know what to call it or even how to explain it, but the feeling is definitely there. We all need to feel loved and accepted. We all crave recognition. Deep down, we all want to make a positive difference. We all have a longing for belonging.

What does this have to do with values and habits? Everything. When we intentionally subject ourselves to a group of likeminded people, who want to live at Level 5, our values change more easily because we have the ultimate support system. Not just mentoring, coaching or consulting. Not just accountability, but a true sense of BElonging. We are a part of something meaningful.

Being part of a community has helped me become the person I wanted to be, to discover who I am and Whose I am, and helps me to continue to BE a better person. I believe we are created to belong to one another. We need each other.

So, if you want to BEcome the person you were created to BE, find a group of people that love you enough to tell you the truth, that care enough about you to hold you accountable, and are committed enough to support you and encourage you. I hope the community you choose will be ours because nothing makes me happier than to watch people grow.

I have a little plaque in my study that says, "Success is making a difference in the lives of others. Happiness is watching them grow because of it." I'm a happy man because I've spent some time on the other side. Instead of being the mentee, I've had the opportunity to be the mentor for many people and I look forward to the millions of people you and I get to touch in the future.

Remember what Frank Outlaw said:

*When you Change your **THINKING**,*

*You Change your **BELIEFS.***

When you Change your beliefs,

*You Change your **EXPECTATIONS**.*

When you Change your expectations,

*You Change your **ATTITUDE**.*

When you Change your attitude,

*You Change your **BEHAVIOR**.*

When you Change your behavior,

*You Change your **PERFORMANCE**.*
When you Change your performance,
*You Change your **LIFE***

*Watch your **THOUGHTS**, they become **WORDS***
*Watch your words, they become **ACTIONS***
*Watch your actions, they become **HABITS***
*Watch your habits, they become your **CHARACTER***
*Watch your character, they determine your **DESTINY***

When you Change your **THINKING**, You Change your **BELIEFS**.

Intentionally thinking about the values you want to live by and being part of a community to support, encourage, and hold you accountable, actually helps you change what you believe. Without critical thinking, you will begin to believe whatever gets put into your mind, whether that is passive conversation or passive television. Once it is in your mind and free to roam around without examination, your beliefs are automatically changed.

When you Change your beliefs, You Change your **EXPECTATIONS**.

When you believe something, you have expectations. If I truly believe that I can reach a goal, I'm going to expect to reach that goal. If you believe that you are truly born to win as Zig says, and you believe that when you plan to win and prepare to win that you can expect to win, your expectations change because of your beliefs.

Super Bowl Champion coach of the Baltimore Colts, Tony Dungee, taught his team that if they did specific things – small things – that developed into habits, that they would win. At first they didn't believe they could win, so they didn't expect to win and they didn't implement the small habits that coach said would give them victory.

When they practiced the small things and began to see them working, their belief (and therefore expectation) increased.

When you Change your expectations, You Change your **ATTITUDE**.

When you believe and expect, you have HOPE. When you don't believe that you will be successful at something, how is your attitude going to be? Zig said "You can't do *anything* with a positive attitude, but you can do *everything* better with a positive attitude than you can with a negative one. Your attitude is connected to your belief."

When you Change your attitude, You Change your **BEHAVIOR**.

If I don't believe I'm going to win – I'm not going to take action. Can you now see how all action is tied to BElief?

When you Change your behavior, You Change your **PERFORMANCE**.

In all areas of life and business, your result is determined by what you DO. I can say I love my wife, but if I don't show it, it means nothing. You've certainly said to someone in the past "actions speak louder than words." What you actually DO proves what you BElieve.

When you Change your performance You Change your **LIFE**

When my performance changes in the seven core areas of life, my life changes. Everyone wants life change. The question is, "Do you BElieve that your life can change? Do you BElieve that it is up to you to change it? What do you THINK about success in life and business?

Watch your **THOUGHTS**, they become **WORDS**

Start by thinking about what you're thinking about. Where do those thoughts come from? Will this thought help you become the person you want to be? Will it help you reach your dreams and goals in life?

Watch your words, they become **ACTIONS**

Someone once said, "We lie loudest when we lie to ourselves." If we are self-aware, we would all admit that we lie to ourselves, but no one wants to be a liar, right? Since you BElieve what you say, every word you say is accepted by your subconscious mind as truth. Therefore, refuse to verbalize negative thoughts. Be realistic, of course, but refuse to speak negative thoughts. Especially about yourself.

Like most people, you probably have some word or phrase that you blurt out when you fail. It might be "I'm so stupid!" or "I'm such an idiot!." When you blame others, you might blurt out the same words toward someone else, or worse, you might verbalize your disgust at God.

Resist the temptation to verbalize negative thoughts. Confess the truth in advance. Activate your faith and your belief will change.

Watch your actions, they become **HABITS**

Remember that the more you do what you do, the more it becomes ingrained in your soul. It creates roadways in your mind and emotions. Everything you do activates dopamine or serotonin, creating deeper grooves in your very being.

Watch your habits, they become your **CHARACTER**

You are where you are today because of your habits. You are who you are today because of your habits. And your habits go all the way back to your beliefs that were shaped by unintentional or intentional thinking.

Watch your character, it determines your **DESTINY**

Where do you want to go? Who do you want to be? Where does God want you to go? Who has God called you to BE? Who you ARE will determine your Destiny.

Who do you think you ARE?

Chapter 9

Phenomenal L.I.F.E. G.O.A.L.S!

Throughout this book, I've reminded you that the process of *The 5 Levels* is nothing more than a muse without attaching them to a meaningful goal. The levels must be in context of a specific outcome, result or goal. With that in mind, we also know that most people don't know how to set goals. So let me share my acronym for L.I.F.E. G.O.A.L.S! with you.

Let's start with L.I.F.E. **Living In Freedom Every** day is understanding that you can be free in your mind and in your heart. When you understand who you are and Whose you are and you understand your purpose and your passion, you'll live a phenomenal life.

It doesn't mean you won't have problems and that you won't have to sacrifice. Look at the perfect model, Jesus. He had to give His very life, but He lived in freedom. His mind and heart were not locked up. He was not shackled by poor thinking and a lack of knowing how to love. He was not bound with emotional turmoil. He knew Who He was and *Whose* He was. He was free even though He allowed Himself to be taken prisoner and killed to accomplish His purpose on earth.

G=GOALS

Many people set goals at the beginning of each year and call them "New Year's Resolutions." By mid-February, they couldn't even tell you what the "resolution" actually was! In fact, it was not a resolution or a decision. It was not even a true intention. It was a wish. It was a mustering of willpower - that's all. Without the continuing inspiration – without a lasting desire - the wish most likely won't come true and if it does, it will be by accident. I don't know about you, but I don't want my success to be by accident. I understand that I cannot control circumstances and I must defer to the Will of God for my life, but I also know that "only a fool would build a tower without a plan."

Even if you didn't make specific resolutions for the New Year, there were probably a few things that crossed your mind that you wanted to change about your life and your business. You probably set some goals. Setting goals should be a lifestyle. Let me say that again, "Setting goals should be a *lifestyle*." What do I mean by that? What I mean is that you should be reflecting on where you are in life and in your business EVERY DAY. How are you going to make that a habit? By going through *The 5 Levels* of course!

You should be looking at your clearly defined written goals EVERY DAY. You may feel that you are not good at setting goals. I disagree. The fact is that almost every person on the planet knows how to set goals. Let me prove it. Do you have a favorite TV show? Do you have a favorite football team? Did you watch the Super Bowl or go to a movie this year? Aha! I would be willing to bet that you know exactly when "your" show or "your" team comes on. And guess what? You rearranged your schedule so that you could be in front of the boob tube! You set a goal and you realized that goal! Now, all you have to do is transfer that same concept to the rest of your life and to your business.

Let's start with your life goals. Life goals are the things you want to achieve in life, whether those things are physical (like losing weight), emotional (like controlling your temper), spiritual (like getting closer to God) or material (owning something you don't currently have). Life goals could incorporate how many hours you work, how much you play sports or travel.

It can be as unique and as extensive as you want. The reason that you want to start with life goals is because your life goals are the only reason your business exists. You went into business for a reason. Do you remember why? Was it to make a lot of money? Are you doing that? Was it to chart your own course – to be your own boss? Are you doing that? Was it to have a little more free time? Are you spending more time with the family?

The greatest lesson you will ever learn in business is that your business exists for one reason and one reason only. It is to be a vehicle to help you achieve your life goals - that's the reason you went into business. You thought going into business for yourself would help you achieve your life goals, more than any other choices you had at the time. Instead, if you are like most small business owners, you got something far different. Instead of having more free time, you work yourself to death. Instead of a business, you have a 24 hour-7 days a week "job." You became a slave to the business. The thing that is now a hungry monster must be fed.

My good friend, best-selling author Michael Gerber, wrote a book called *The E-Myth*, which reveals how people go into business with dreams of success only to become slaves of the business. They think that because they do the "technical" part of the business well, they will automatically be successful in business. This is a deadly assumption. Because they spend all their time "doing" the work of the business (working "in" it), they don't spend enough time working "on" it such as planning, marketing, and building systems so that the owner is not required for the business to run.

This is not to say that you cannot work in your business and it certainly doesn't mean that every business has to grow beyond the owner. It just means that if you want to use your business as a vehicle to achieve your life goals - and it's not currently doing that - then something has to change. In order to create change, you have to have a vision, which means you will have to set some goals for yourself and for your business.

So, in order to reach your goal of going into business (like taking a certain amount of time off), it's going to require some work "on" the business. It will take planning rather than simply letting things happen by accident. Success doesn't happen by accident. It happens by intentionally focusing on what it is you want, outlining a plan and implementing that plan.

"Without clearly defined goals, you will never know where you are going and when and if you ever get there." – Chuck Coonradt

---

You cannot hit a target that you cannot see. If you succeed without goals, then it is by accident - and that's scary! The reason that succeeding by accident is a problem is because you don't know how to duplicate that success in the future. By setting goals, you have a target. You *know* what you are shooting for. You will develop strategies to reach the goal. If successful, then you can duplicate the recipe again and again.

Not having goals greatly reduces your chance of success. I have a photograph of a basketball goal in my office. The caption says, "You will miss 100% of the shots you do not take." How true. Could you imagine a ballgame without goals? How would you know who won and when the game was over? The game of business has a scoreboard. By setting goals, you can know how you are doing in the game.

Ball games are won by reaching more goals than the competition. You may have direct competitors in your industry, but your biggest competitor is probably the one that greets you in the mirror each morning! Someone once said, "We have seen the enemy and he is us!" Often, we set ourselves up for failure simply by doing nothing. Failure doesn't require doing anything. My waistline will continue to grow unless I do something. If I don't set food intake goals (or limits in this case) and exercise goals, then my waistline will grow all by itself. Success in business does not happen by accident – it happens by design.

5 Steps to Reaching Your Goals

As I mentioned earlier, setting goals should be a lifestyle. Set 12-month goals, 30-day goals and "today" goals. Your today goals are on your Daily Action List. Determine where you want to be 12 months from now, both personally and in your small business. Then, break it down into months. What needs to be done in the next 30 days? Write out the action steps that are required for each goal. The first action step of each goal should be on your daily action list. Look at this list EVERY DAY and re-prioritize and implement the list every day.

Step 1: Set SMART Goals
SMART GOALS

S – Specific. Have specific goals. Don't be general. If it is money, be specific about exactly how much. Your goals shouldn't be defined by "more" or "bigger," being very specific will make it more likely that you will reach the goal.

M – Measurable. You can't manage what can't be measured. A goal is not a goal unless it can somehow be measured. If it is a physical goal, it can be measured in weight or body fat. A financial goal can be measured easily. Production goals can be measured. Even habit goals can be measured. For example, let's say you're building a habit of loving your spouse. You can count the number of times you give a gift, share a word of encouragement, or provide an act of service.

A – Attainable. The difference between a dream and a goal is that a dream is inspiring a picture of the future – the almost unattainable. Goals are the mile-markers to get you there. It's very important to have short-term goals. Determine the very first step - the smaller the better. Studies have proven that small wins are the beginning of changing habits. Small wins create momentum and belief. Consistent base hits turn into runs. First downs turn into touchdowns. Focus on the small wins every day.

R – Relative. Your goals should be relative to your dream. Your daily goals should help you reach your weekly goals, which helps you reach your monthly goals, annual goals, and life goals – your dream. Make sure your goals fit with your overall vision. Last year I worked on bottling my own Caesar Salad dressing because it's the best on earth. I got my favorite store to agree to sell it, contacted a bottling company and so on. After investing some time on it, I realized that my other important goals that have more to do with my overall life goals weren't getting the attention they deserved. I quickly abandoned the Caesar Salad dressing idea, for now - I'll come back to it because it's something I want to do for myself, but it isn't relative to my overall goals. Remember, we have to stay focused! Be willing to say "no" to a lot of "good" things, so you can focus on the "best" things.

T – Time sensitive. Goals need completion dates to create a sense of urgency. Have a specific date of when that goal is to be realized.

Step 2: Have the End in Sight

"Begin with the end in mind" is one of the late Stephen Covey's seven habits in the best-selling *7 Habits of Highly Successful People.* The only way to set a specific goal is to see the end as it is. You have to have vision.

You need to see as many parts as possible. In other words, if I set a goal to take my business to a certain dollar amount, it means that I will have a certain number of people on staff. It means I will need to take specific action in my marketing plan to take my business there. It may mean that I need more equipment, and so on. The point is that you can't just list the specific goal without taking into consideration what else will be involved.

You will never know all of the dynamics of how it will be and what you will experience once you get there, but you need to have an idea of what is absolutely required to be there. For example, when I took my first business to over $2 million per year, I had the end in sight. I knew that I would need a certain number of people, etc., but what I didn't know was how it would *feel.* I didn't realize what I would learn leading 33 people.

I didn't understand management dynamics as I do now; I have experienced it firsthand. I knew how to manage a staff of seven, but a group of thirty-three and working with middle management was a totally new experience. So you won't always know what kind of experiences you will have along the way. That's why we say that success is a journey – not a destination. It is the life lessons we learn along the way that create the real success and not just reaching the goal. However, the only way to get on the journey is to set our sights on a destination.

"It's not what you get when you reach your goals, it's what you become"
– Zig Ziglar

Step 3: Write Down Your Goals

I know. I know. You've probably heard this from every motivational speaker you've ever heard! I wonder why? Could it be because it works?! Maybe they are paid speakers because they have reached a few goals in their lives? We all know that it works, but *why* does it work? Believe it or not, everyone has a "photographic" memory. Some are just longer than others! Your subconscious mind takes "pictures" of whatever you see every day. It burns into your subconscious mind so that you take action on your goals even when you are not thinking about them.

Also, your body learns through repetition. I like to write my goals over and over - not like a chant, but just defining and refining, thinking and reflecting. I have a permanent place for them, but I am always reviewing them, thus, re-writing them. A third reason that writing your goal down works is due to the fact that the "written" word is more powerful than the "spoken" word. Your employees should know what the "community" goals are and what their specific goals are to help achieve that, whether it is sales performance, production, re- services, or whatever. They should be posted and communicated EVERY DAY.

Step 4: Break it Down

Once you have set a specific goal in time and number, break it down by the year, month, week and day. For example, let's say your goal is to save $50,000.00 in the next five years. That's $10K per year, $833.00 per month, approximately $192.00 per week, and $32.00 per day on a 6-day workweek. Although $50,000.00 can seem daunting, increasing your income by $32.00 a day doesn't sound too difficult.

Step 5: Review and Adjust Regularly

Step 5: Review and Adjust Regularly: Your goals will change. Your worldview will change. You need to check to see how your strategies are working, so look at your goals EVERY DAY.

9 Reasons People Don't Reach Their Goals
Reason #1: No Burning Desire

In the timeless classic, *Think and Grow Rich*, Napoleon Hill says, "You must have a burning desire." Zig Ziglar said that the #1 ingredient for success is *desire*. If you don't have desire - if you can't see it, and it's not compelling enough for YOU to get out of YOUR comfort zone - you won't get there.

The reason for lack of desire is the absence of a dream.

Reason # 2: The "I Can't" Factor

In the movie "The Edge," a deep thinking billionaire, played by Anthony Hopkins, and an immature fashion photographer, played by Alec Baldwin, were stranded in the Alaskan wilderness after their seaplane crashed in a lake. Two of their colleagues were killed in the crash and one had been eaten by a bear. The same bear is now stalking them.

Hungry, cold and exhausted, Alec Baldwin was overcome by fear and began to crumble under the pressure. Anthony Hopkins had read books on how people survived difficult conditions and chose to focus on the solution rather than the problem.

He insisted that his unbelieving co-star repeat over and over again "What one man can do, another can do!" Do yourself a favor – take the two words "I can't" out of your vocabulary. Your words have power. Many people are programmed from a very early age with an "I can't" program. "You can't do that…" we were told. Deep down, this file is still replaying in our subconscious. We must defeat the negative self-talk with the positive "I can, and God willing, I will!"

If you believe you can, you will. If you don't, you won't.

Reason # 3: Circumstances.

Another convenient way of cheating ourselves out of success is blaming our woes on circumstances. People make excuses because of some event or some other person. I have two words to rebut this stinkin' thinkin': Helen Keller. Helen Keller was deaf, dumb and blind, but she managed to become a best-selling author, a speaker and an American legend. She didn't let her circumstances keep her from having a positive impact on the world. Many times, difficult circumstances can create successful opportunities that could never be realized otherwise. None of us like the thought of "rejoicing in our tribulations," but trials build patience and character.

A friend of ours' husband committed adultery. They had two young kids, a business, and two homes. Her dream was dashed. He ruined his life. She can allow this to ruin hers too or she can stay focused on her dreams and goals and rise above the circumstances. You don't know what will be presented to you on this journey called life. Bad things happen. It's how we respond to them that makes the difference.

Reason # 4: People.

The people who influence your life can *encourage* you or *discourage* you. Where do you get your worldview from? Are those that are most influential in your life helping or hurting? Stay away from negative people that bring you down. If you have to be around them, rebuff their negativity with positive affirmations. Throw out the newspaper and pick up some inspirational materials. Avoid the media, the Internet news services, and fill your mind with positive, inspiring thoughts.

Build a team of people around you that includes mentors, coaches, peer groups and team members - people that can see you and see what you are doing from the outside rather than the inside, and people that encourage you, not discourage you.

SPECIAL NOTE: If you have to be around people who are negative, don't try to change them unless they want your help. Instead, take the position that you refuse to be changed by them if they don't have your best interest at heart. You don't have to respond or try to convince them. Just smile in your heart because you know who you are, Whose you are and what you can do.

Those who are close to you that don't want you to be successful are not bad people or do they hate you. They know that if you are successful, they will have to come out of their comfort zone. They have the "fear of success." The fear of success is the same as the fear of failure.

You see, to be successful, you have to fail. On the climb to success, you have the Success Zone on top, the Comfort Zone in the middle, and the

Failure Zone at rock bottom. No one wants to fail, but if you play to win, you will fail at some things. Failure is not a person; it's an event. It's an event that does not have to be repeated.

Your DREAM TEAM is vital to your success. There are people in your life that don't understand your dream. Sometimes it's those that are closest to you. "Who do you think YOU are?" is their question. "Why would you want to risk the life you have?" Don't allow negative thinkers to influence you. At the same time, don't feel the need to convince them of the validity of your dream. If it's a good dream, God will see it through. If it's not, you'll learn your lesson.

When I first started Phenomenal Products, I produced three small manuals that became my first product. These manuals showed "mom-and-pop" businesses how to grow to their first million.

The set of manuals was $199.00. When I told some of my family members what I was doing, they looked confused. One of my brothers asked, "Let me get this straight. You're selling *photocopies* for 200 bucks?" (Of course the value is in the information, not in the value of the paper!).

Although he is a very successful business owner, he didn't get it. His view was that I should focus on the one local service business I had and do that for the rest of my life. That approach has been very successful for him, but it's not the right road for a dreamer like me. Now that I'm working with some of the top business trainers in the world, he sees the life change that has taken place with my coaching members and that my local service company continues to thrive without me working in it every day. He understands and is very proud of me.

You need to know who you are and what your purpose and calling are. John Maxwell says, "You have to know yourself to grow yourself." If you're a restless, hopeless dreamer like me, this book is for you. If you aren't but you need to rise above average thinking so that you can make better choices, this book will help you THINK about your life so that you can BEcome the person you are supposed to BE - the person you were created to be.

Of course, we must include our spouse and children in our dreams and our goals. It must be fair to all involved. Sometimes you have to temper your dreams to accommodate those God has given you. Don't worry about what others think, but our biggest dreams in life should be to love God and love our families. Even if we have to give up our biggest lifestyle desires because our spouse isn't ready, that is okay.

For example, as I write this piece, I'm in Greece with friends and my wife is back home in the U.S. I was invited to London to speak at Cambridge University with Tom Ziglar. Since I was going to be in Europe, I wanted to go someplace I ordinarily wouldn't get to go, being so far from the U.S. Our friends were going to be in Greece and we have an open invitation. What a PHENOMENAL place to relax, think and write!

If my wife wasn't okay with it, I would have to be okay with that. The reason for failed relationships is selfishness.

The growth and maturity you get from that is what marriage is all about. On the other hand, don't limit God; He can do miracles. One of the things I am so grateful for is that my wife also fell in love with Destin and was on board with my dream. She is secure with who she is, so I have a lot of freedom to travel and do things that perhaps others wouldn't be able to.

Reason # 5: The Wrong Goals

Everyone has goals. I love the television show *Shark Tank*. I love it because I love small business and there are great lessons revealed on the show. Every Friday night, I have a goal to watch that show. If you plan to be in front of the TV to watch a ballgame or your favorite show, that's a goal. You can set a goal to engage in the meaningless chatter about what's happening in the media or you can set a goal to make a difference in others lives. You can set a goal to be what others want you to be or you can set goals that will help you reach your dream. It's up to you. You have goals. Everyone does. You just have to set the right ones. You have to decide.

Reason # 6: FEAR

Fear is another reason goals aren't met - the fear of failure, the fear of success, and the fear of the unknown. Do you know the acronym for FEAR?

False

Evidence

Appearing

Real

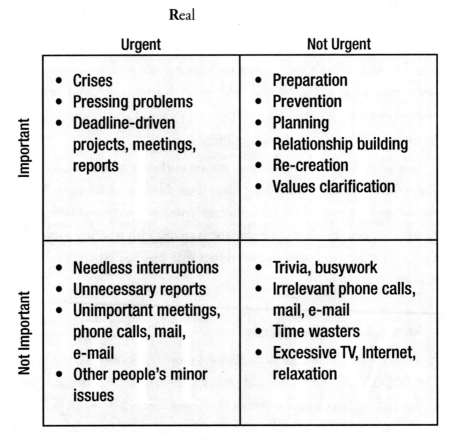

	Urgent	Not Urgent
Important	• Crises • Pressing problems • Deadline-driven projects, meetings, reports	• Preparation • Prevention • Planning • Relationship building • Re-creation • Values clarification
Not Important	• Needless interruptions • Unnecessary reports • Unimportant meetings, phone calls, mail, e-mail • Other people's minor issues	• Trivia, busywork • Irrelevant phone calls, mail, e-mail • Time wasters • Excessive TV, Internet, relaxation

God gave us a phenomenal imagination, but we use it the wrong way. Instead of using it to dream, we imagine worst things that could happen. Instead of allowing fear to grip you, invest some time thinking clearly and critically. Get your dream team involved to help you evaluate your goals and to see them through.

Reason # 7: Poor Self Image

Zig said, "People don't reach their goals because of a poor self-image." If you don't get anything else from this book, please get this: You ARE a phenomenal product. You were born to win. You are designed for accomplishment, engineered for success, and endowed with the seeds of greatness. After all, God don't make any junk! What one man (or woman) can do, another can do!

Reason # 8: Haven't Been Sold

Zig said that, "Some people just haven't been told they need goals to win in life." Some don't understand that success doesn't happen by accident. The first law in John Maxwell's book, *The 15 Invaluable Laws of Growth*, is the Law of Intentionality. Growth and success don't just happen. Incidentally, the second law is the Law of Awareness. You'll find that many other authors, experts, and huge studies, have validated the things I'm sharing in this book.

Reason #9: Don't Know How

Zig also said, "Some people just don't know how." You need to have a goals system. The Ziglar Planner using my personal organization system shared below will serve you well.

O = ORGANIZATION

The second step in the GOALS! SYSTEM is Organization. Once you have your goals in place, you need to organize them. Small business owners report that one of their biggest challenges is staying organized. So, I decided to share with you my personal organizational system that had done wonders for me and many of my coaching clients.

To stay focused, commit to what I call *The Daily Time Capsule.* Many years ago, I began to take an hour a day to work on my projects, early in the morning when everyone else was asleep. During this "capsule" of time, I don't answer phone calls, check e-mail or surf the Internet. It is completely dedicated to determining what action needs to be taken on my goals. I don't do chores around the house or get distracted with entertainment. This is the time to work ON the business. The only person that can find me is my wife.

I began this procedure when I ran my first business; I had to be at the shop at 7:30am, which meant I had to be up at 5am. I'm an early riser, so it was okay with me. I had big dreams, so I had the inspiration to do what was needed. Don't underestimate the value in being inspired about your vision. If you aren't inspired, you won't implement! It's that simple. Keep dreaming until you get the vision that inspires you. Zig always said that the number one ingredient for success is desire. Desire comes from an inspirational vision.

When I started Phenomenal Products, the goal was to write a few manuals, which were to be my first products. In addition to working on the projects for my business (working on policies and procedures), I wanted to create these manuals. So, for about six weeks I got up at 4am instead of 5.

WARNING: When you get really inspired and excited, you might have trouble sleeping! Sometimes I woke up at 3am and couldn't go back to sleep, so I would get up and begin writing. I finished those manuals in six weeks and launched Phenomenal Products.

I still use the procedure today. My routine after I wake up is to get coffee, read a chapter from the Word of God, pray, and then write for an hour or two. Then, I begin working on my projects. This happens six days a week no matter what. The only exception is if I'm training that day, I'll do a short Time Capsule and may not do any significant writing. I'll spend an hour on moving my projects forward, which involves delegating by e-mail, creating presentations, writing scripts, ads, policies and procedures, communicating with partners, or what have you.

How the Time Capsule Works

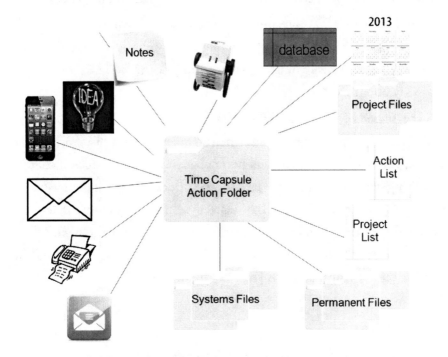

Every day, a whirlwind of "stuff" comes at you. Phone calls, mail, faxes, e-mails and if you're like me, you make a lot of notes and write down ideas. In fact, make sure you do that. That is part of the Thinking/ Dreaming process.

Instead of immediately *reacting* to everything that comes across your desk, prioritize what you are going to focus on. In his best-selling book, *The 7 Habits of Highly Successful People*, Stephen Covey shared a powerful illustration for increasing productivity.

The boxes in the Covey Quadrant are Urgent, Non-Urgent, Important and Non-Important. The idea is to first, put everything in the proper box. Something urgent and important to someone else may not be urgent or important to you.

The idea of The Daily Time Capsule is to prioritize your projects and plan the actions you'll take. Many people burn a great deal of time and energy on the Urgent but Non-Important. Things that are important, but not urgent can easily become urgent if we don't plan and prepare.

John Maxwell says, "Give me just one day with any person and I'll tell you their potential for success." Although that sounds a little arrogant, your daily habits reveal your true values and priorities. Here's what John has to say about it:

"The secret of your success is determined by your daily agenda. If you make a few key decisions and then manage them well in your daily agenda, you will succeed. You will never change your life until you change something you do daily. You see, success, doesn't just suddenly occur one day in someone's life. For that matter, neither does failure. Each is a process. Every day of your life is merely preparation for the next. What you become is the result of what you do today." Zig Ziglar said, "Run your life with a vision and run your day by the clock."

Eat that Frog

All of us have big projects or difficult things we have to face in life. Zig always said, "Eat the big ugly frog first." Brian Tracy wrote a whole book on the subject. You see? We can easily fill our time with the things that are easy and pleasurable. When you get the hard things done first, the rest of your day will go much better.

Big Rocks, Little Rocks

Have you ever seen the demonstration of the big rocks, small rocks, pebbles, sand and water in a container? The big rocks represent the most important things that need to be done, the urgent and important. The smaller rocks represent the lesser important, and so on with the water being the least important of all.

If you put the water in first, then the sand, then the pebbles, then the small rocks, you'll never get the big rocks in the container, but if you start with the big rocks and work your way down, it's amazing how you can work the pebbles, sand and water around the big rocks and small rocks.

Your priorities are the same way. There are things that are easier to do and more fun to do, but you've got to prioritize them and do big rocks first. You've got to eat that frog and get it behind you. This takes a tremendous amount of determination, but remember you can train yourself to make the discipline a habit. And remember what your reward is. Keep the dream alive in your mind every day and every moment.

Each day, during your Daily Time Capsule, you process all of these items. Of course, you are going to take care of the urgent and important things throughout the day, but just because someone else thinks something is important and urgent doesn't mean that it is.

Put all of the items that come across your desk in an Action Folder, if you are mobile. If you work from a desk every day, just put it all in a single stack. When the mail comes, just drop it in the folder or put it on the pile. The reason you get distracted is because you haven't exercised self-control to ignore the piece of mail that's going to steal the time, energy and emotion that could be used to work on your dreams and goals.

During your Daily Time Capsule, you process the Action Folder. The goal of the Daily Time Capsule is two-fold: One, take action on your top projects and two, take action on the whirlwind items. Everything has a destination. During your Daily Time Capsule session, you will actually empty your folder and move everything *somewhere*. The reason this is important is because we will now be able to get them in a place where they can be processed at the optimum time in order to increase your productivity.

Let's start with your projects first since they are the drivers to this system. I teach our small business clients to have four projects. We call them the "phenomenal four." Assuming you have done the thinking, dreaming and planning that you need to do, you will choose your phenomenal four projects. Every day you take action on those projects until they are completed.

For example, let's say your project is to write a sales script. Each day, you will take some action toward that; it should be measurable. Perhaps you do what I do and schedule an hour or so to write every day. You keep that project on the list until it is completed, then add another project in it's place. Your Projects are the things you've identified that will bring you closer to your goal. Projects are multi-step processes. Once completed, they will help you go to the next level. For example, the book I am writing right now is a project. Each day, I work on it and get closer to completion. Completing this project gets me closer to my goal of helping more people get what they want out of life.

Other examples include creating a business plan or a marketing campaign. It might be planning an event. The key is to determine what the *most important* projects are. It can be a challenge because everything seems urgent and important, but you must choose because working on too many projects at once dilutes your energy and focus and they may never get completed.

Choosing the right projects to focus on requires that you do an assessment. The Wheel of Life is a great tool for seeing where you are in life, and determining what you need to focus on. We also have a Wheel of Business so you can see where your business is right now.

My experience has been that most people don't know how to properly assess where they are. They want to believe that they are doing better than they are or they focus on what they haven't done, rather than the progress they've made.

It reminds me of something my early mentor Bill Beckham taught me: "Most people fall in one of two ditches: The ditch of pride, or the ditch of guilt." The place to start is reality. This is why assessments are so critical. Assessing your communication style with D.I.S.C. or some type of behavior assessment shows you how you are hard-wired. Facing reality is the first step toward phenomenal success! Get real with yourself and others. Then, FOCUS on the things that are true and that will help you move forward. Choose your projects wisely! Get with your coach. Moving through *The 5 levels* requires support, encouragement and accountability.

Ask yourself these questions:

What is going to have the biggest impact in my business over the next 90 days?

What will have the biggest impact on my personal life over the next 90 days?

What should the focus areas be?

You will need and want to get advice from your Dream Team (your spouse, coaches, mentors and staff) to determine what the most important items are.

Processing the Action Folder

In each Time Capsule session, you will empty the folder (or get to the bottom of the pile). If you do this every day, it's not a chore. Everything has a destination.

Let's start with the Project Folders - physical folders and electronic folders. You might even have an e-mail folder for each of your projects. I have a Project Folder right now for this book. As I get ideas, suggestions, research results or anything else related to the completion this book, it goes in that Project Folder.

Then, I work on that folder during my Time Capsule. What is the next action step? Right now, the only action step is "WRITE!" Next, I'll do more research and make some more edits. I take action until it's done, which brings me to another piece of the system...

The Action List. The ONLY things that go on this list are things that will be done TODAY. Avoid overloading your Action List (I'm guilty!). Your Action List can be in a spiral notebook, a planner like the Ziglar planner, or on your electronic calendar, which is where I want to go next...

Your Calendar. As you work your Action Folder, there will be things that need to be scheduled. Phenomenally successful people run their life by a calendar!

Then, you process all the other items in your **Action Folder:**

E-mail: Is it urgent? If not, flag it and come back to it later.

Mail and Faxes: Do you have to respond now? If not, put it in a folder. For example, I pay my personal bills once a month. I just stick the mail in a folder and once a month, I pay them online. It takes about 15 minutes a month. You could do that weekly or even daily, but the idea is that it is organized.

Phone calls: If you are in a situation where you have clients calling you directly and you need to take those calls, avoid them during your Daily Time Capsule. The main benefit of The Daily Time Capsule is to get the important things behind you so you can work "in" the business the rest of the day.

Personally, I almost never answer my phone unless I know who it is or I have an appointment with them. Schedule all of your activities in time blocks. When do you take appointments? When do you meet with your staff? When do you exercise? Schedule all of it. I take and return calls when I'm in the car. I have hands-free, Bluetooth; I think it's the best time because when I'm in front of my computer, I can do more productive things.

My coaching calls, webinars, etc. are all scheduled at strategic times of the day. Everything is scheduled and planned. If you are in a business and you are the Operations Manager, then your time has to be open to deal with the brush fires until you get someone to replace you. The brush fires have to be dealt with. The only question is do you have to be the one doing it.

I love the acronym DEAL in Tim Ferris' book, *The 4 Hour Work Week.* D stands for Delegate, E stands for Eliminate, A equals Automate and L is for Liberate. Always ask yourself, "Can someone else do this? Can

I streamline it? Can I eliminate it?" As a business owner, you should be aware of your hourly worth. Avoid doing $20.00 an hour work when you're worth $200!

For each project, you will have a Project File. The things you are going to do TODAY go on your Action List.

A = ACTION

The third step is to take massive action. The reason that most small businesses don't grow or do as well as they could is because of F.T.I. (Failure To Implement)! Would you agree that just getting the things you know you need to get done would make you more successful? You bet! So, the more productive you are, the more action you take, and the more successful you become.

Let's go back and review where we started in this book. When you change your thinking, you change your beliefs. When you change your beliefs, you change your expectations. When you change your expectations, you change your attitude. When you change your attitude, you change your behavior (ACTION). When you change your behavior, you change your performance. When you change your performance, you change your life. True or true?

I can tell my wife how much I love her, but until I actually DO something, it's not real. A Japanese proverb says, "Vision without action is a daydream." Nothing happens until something happens! The rest of the proverb says, "Action without vision is a nightmare." You see? You are DOING something, but are your actions in line with your vision? A phenomenal vision plus a phenomenal action equals phenomenal success!

You can have the best ideas, the most knowledge and all the understanding, but if you don't DO anything, it's worthless. The difference between successful people and unsuccessful people is what they DO and don't DO. Not that they just can't, they won't; and remember that DOING is a result of BEING.

L = LEARNING

Once you set your goals, organize your plan and take action, you must LEARN from the results. What worked? What didn't? How is your awareness level as you focus on taking action? What level are you in? Be objective. Be honest. Educate yourself so that you won't make the same mistakes over and over. Albert Einstein said, "The definition of insanity is doing the same thing the same way over and over expecting a different result."

S = SYSTEMS

"S" stands for SYSTEMS. Once you observe what works, put it into a system. Once you have reached your goal of losing weight, getting more customers, increasing your profit or whatever, make it an AUTOMATIC way of life. DUPLICATE IT, AUTOMATE IT, and DELEGATE IT. By all means DON'T REINVENT IT!

The ground-breaking book, *The Power of Habit,* proves through numerous clinical studies that one of the key points in changing habits is changing the routine. The cue and the reward may stay the same, but remember that changing the routine (the system) is the easiest part. When you have a dream (the reward) and you train yourself on a new routine (a system), you have a better chance of reaching your goal.

A system is simply a way of doing something that delivers predictable results. For example, if I have a system of eating certain things at certain times, I will lose weight. If I work out for a specific amount of time for a specific period in a specific way, I will build muscles in the intended area. The same is true for any goal. If I want to write a 200-page book and my system is to write one page per day and I stick to that system, I *will* have a 200-page book in 200 days - simple as that.

Systems don't have to be complicated. In fact, my good friend and successful business consultant Ellen Rohr says, "The simpler you make it, the farther you can take it." Your scheduling is a system. Your exercise and eating routine is a system. The way you make money is a system. Learning can be a system. Systematize your life and your business, so that you can get more done. That's what systems do.

In risking repeating my other two books, let me give you a crash course in systems. It bears repeating because most people don't implement systems even after they hear about them!

There are five components of a system: Your mission, your organizational chart, your policies, your procedures and your job descriptions. You can systematize your company with those five things. Learn about that in my book, *The 5 Secrets of a Phenomenal Business*.

Your mission is what you are trying to accomplish every day. It's the strategy to fulfill your vision - this could be a company mission or a personal mission. My dream is for the entire world to live in a community; in other words, everyone on the planet has a support system and they've learned to be open and real with themselves and others. They've learned what you are learning here – that a phenomenally successful person is one who is diligent and focused – one who runs their life with a vision instead of by circumstance. Of course, we all know that the dream will never come true. It's an impossible dream, but when you have a big dream – one that is inspiring, but impossible - it gives you a big vision.

My vision is to have small groups meeting in every major city in the world supporting one another and experiencing a sense of community. The vision is real. That can happen and it is happening already. We have people meeting in groups over the phone from Australia, UK, Canada and the U.S.

My mission is to create community in every enterprise I create. Our mission in my coaching program is to create a phenomenal community experience. Why? Because it has been proven that when people feel like they belong to a community, change happens more rapidly. They have the support, the encouragement and the accountability they need - that is not just my opinion. Huge studies have been done that are referenced in *The Power of Habit*. Every company that I own lives with a sense of community – a sense of shared vision, values, mission and purpose.

My purpose is to help members of my communities create L.I.F.E. (Living In Freedom Every day), not only in their own lives, but in all the lives they touch.

The Organizational Chart shows the functions of the organization - who does what. Every business, every event and every organization has different functions that must be fulfilled in order to achieve the goal. A sports team has positions each with a different role. In your own life, if you want to be phenomenally successful, you need a team. If you try to do everything yourself, you won't be able to grow to the level you need to grow.

Personally, I have systems in place so that I can leverage my time and focus on the most important, the biggest impact, and highest return possible activities. We have someone that cleans our home and takes care of it (and our dogs) when we travel. I have my dry cleaning delivered. Someone else cuts my grass, cleans the pool, etc. When I've done it myself it has been a disaster. I've figured out how to pay someone else twenty bucks an hour so I can focus on building something that is not only worth much more, but will make a difference in the world.

Don't let me confuse you. There are plenty of people who cut their own grass that are successful. If you want to live a different life, you can, but you need infrastructure to do it. When I travel, I still spend time checking my own e-mail and responding to text messages, but I decided on this trip to Grand Cayman, that I would let my staff do that. I just take text messages from my assistant Michelle. They check my e-mail and my voicemail so that I can focus on finishing this book and enjoy the time here.

Each person involved in this particular case has a "job description." Our housekeeper knows what to do. My staff knows what is required of them. You simply delegate everything you can to others.

Then, you have policies and procedures they use to make sure we get the consistent results needed to reach the goal. My companies continue to hit record sales and profits because of the systems that we've set up and worked on for many years.

Policies are in place just like boundaries and rules guide a football game. There are proven, practiced and rehearsed procedures that consistently give the right results. Once you observe what they are (awareness) and you are willing to change and commit to them, systems will serve you very well. To quote my good friend David Frey one more time, "Will power is for losers, systems are for winners."

Procedures are the *how* to do something. Simple, step-by-step instructions on how to do a specific task.

! = INSPIRATION!

Finally, the "!" stands for INSPIRATION. The reason most small business owners are not successful is *not* because they don't know what to do. **It's simply because they just don't do it**. I find that those who are excited about what they are doing – those who are inspired by the possibilities – can't wait to get going each day. They are the ones that actually DO what needs to be done to take their business and their lives to the next level.

They are INSPIRED to implement. They BElieve. People who are discouraged become depressed; therefore they don't take action. People, who are not inspired, don't implement. They do just enough to avoid the pain of total failure, but not enough to rise above mediocrity. So how does one become inspired?

By getting a vision for your life. By dreaming. You create desire through intentional dreaming. You should be inspired by the fact, the truth, that you ARE phenomenal and you CAN do phenomenal things and you CAN have a phenomenal L.I.F.E. If that doesn't get you excited, nothing will.

When I talk about inspiration, I don't mean just a moment of vision or some phenomenon that occurs once in a while or even conjuring up "energy" from the universe. What I mean is the KNOWING who you ARE and WHOSE you are – having the joy of knowing that you are, therefore you can. Inspiration is BElieving. It's Believing in God. It's Believing the truth. It's Believing that you can.

Chapter 10

Your Phenomenal Spiritual Identity

You would probably agree that humans are made up of spirit, soul and body. We usually think of ourselves in terms of being a body with a soul and a spirit, but we are *spirit* first. I've heard it put this way - we are a spirit wearing an "earth suit." Kind of like an astronaut, he is wearing a space suit so that he can function in the space environment. The suit is not him.

Since we are spirit, soul and body, and our values are wrapped up in our beliefs, ignoring the spiritual aspect of who we are would be akin to malpractice. Separating who we are spiritually, emotionally and mentally would be like trying to separate oil and water after they've been mixed.

But I have a bit of a challenge. Not everyone sees "spirituality" the same way, which puts me in a position of either ignoring the subject altogether or trying to appease everyone. Since I cannot separate who I am spiritually and physically – it's all one package – I'm going to share this point of view from the perspective of a believer in Jesus Christ.

Based on that, you can decide whether you want to read this chapter or not. We all agree that what we think about God will have a dramatic impact on our lives. We just can't agree on Who He is.

We may not even agree that God exists. Many people think it's not politically correct, or polite to talk about God. Especially Jesus! It seems that it's okay to laugh at a Christian's belief, but we can't challenge the dominant thought of the day. I'm willing to risk telling you the truth at the expense of what you may think about me because I *know* who I am and Whose I am.

So, shouldn't I be *inclusive* and *tolerant*? On the idea of tolerance, I'll quote my good friend Tom Ziglar… "Would you rather have me *tolerate* you or *love* you?"

The first thing you must understand is that Christianity is *not* a religion and it is *not* inclusive. Jesus said, "I am the Way, the Truth and the Life. No man comes to the Father but by Me." He also said, "Before Abraham was, I AM." Many times in Scripture, Jesus revealed that He was the ONLY Son of God and he was the ONLY way to God.

Former atheist, legendary Christian author C.S. Lewis wrote, "If Jesus really said that, then He was either a liar, a lunatic, or Lord." He either knew He wasn't the Son of God and lied about it, He was deceived and just thought He was Lord, or He really is.

I also understand that many so called Christian religions have done a lot of damage in the world and continue to do so. To ignore Christianity because of what others have done is like refusing to drive because others have been killed by drunk drivers.

So, what Christianity teaches is that there are only two kinds of people in the world:

1. You ARE a Christian believer. You believe that Jesus Christ is the Son of God and the only way to God the Father is through Him. If that is the case, this chapter may be the most important thing you've ever read. As a Christian believer, who wasn't very successful BEing a Christian, the truths in this chapter changed my life.

2. You don't believe that Jesus Christ is the only way to God. I meet people who would say something like "I don't want to limit myself," "It's not possible that there is only one way," or "No one can know who God really is." If that's you, take the lessons from the previous chapters. They will serve you well. You can ignore this chapter if you like.

If this chapter speaks to you, then wonderful! I'm open to learning from people who don't believe like I do all the time. If you are open to a conversation on faith, I would be happy to have that conversation with you. You can also read my testimony in my first book, *7 Secrets of a Phenomenal L.I.F.E.,* or online at www.HowardPartridge.org.

Please don't judge true Christians by the few religious bigots or the mass of people who carry the label, but don't live it out. Maybe they just don't know who they are yet! If that's the case, give them a copy of this book!

The Christian Believer's TRUE Identity

After I came to know God, I did what I thought a Christian was supposed to do - go to church all the time, preach to other people, and point out their sin. Meanwhile, I wasn't really successful overcoming my own shortcomings. Many Christians live powerless lives and that sense of helplessness is constantly reinforced with statements such as "after all, we're all sinners" or "we're just sinners saved by grace." What's worse is that many religions teach that you have to do more good works to be forgiven or accepted. Nothing could be farther from the truth.

I have come to believe that being a Christian isn't about religion, but about a relationship. As we begin to understand WHO WE ARE in Christ, everything changes. The revelation came to me one night as my pastor and I were washing dishes. Our wives were enjoying after dinner coffee in the living room; we were serving them by cleaning up.

I shared a struggle that I was having at the time. I don't remember what it was now, but I'll never forget the conversation that followed. "Why do you think that is?" he asked. "Because I have a wicked heart." I said. "What do you mean?" he asked curiously. "Well, the book of Jeremiah says 'the heart of man is desperately wicked, who can know it'. I have a wicked mind. All of us do." "No you don't." he said. "You have the mind of Christ. Because you are saved, you've been freed. You've been made a new creature. You are no longer who you were. The old man is gone."

Obviously confused, I asked "Then why do people sin?" "Because Christians don't know who they are!" he laughed. "And when we do know, we sometimes forget!" he said with a big belly laugh. He then introduced me to a book called *Victory Over Darkness* by Neil Anderson where I found out about the work of Bill and Annabel Gillham. They wrote a book called *Lifetime Guarantee* and recorded a DVD/CD program called *The Life* based on Galatians 2:20

I have been crucified with Christ; and it is no longer I who live, but Christ lives in me; and the life which I now live in the flesh I live by faith in the Son of God, who loved me and gave Himself up for me.

From that point on, I *knew who I was*! Because of that, I knew that nothing I did (or didn't do) could improve my position with Christ! I could not earn His favor. Sure, when you sin, there are always consequences, but the *reason* you sin is because you forget WHO you ARE in Christ! Is there more to it than that? Of course.

It's a process of BEcoming.

It's a process of BEcoming the person you already ARE in Christ and allowing Him to live through you. As Bill Gillham says, "The Christian life is not difficult to live. It's impossible. Only one person has ever lived it and only one person will ever live it, and that is Christ *through* you."

Once I learned this, I noticed many Scriptures that deal with the identity of a Christian believer. They began to jump off the page. I read a number of books on the subject and even had a few arguments with fellow believers of whether we are "sinner or saint." I read a chapter from the New Testament every day and have done so for almost 25 years.

A couple of years ago, I decided the next time I went through The New Testament, I would record every Scripture I could find on our identity in Christ. I started in Romans because in the Gospels and part of Acts, Jesus had not risen and the Holy Spirit had not come. I may have missed some Scriptures too. This was simply done as a personal project and not to be the "end all" of the subject. Please understand I am not a scholar, a pastor or a spiritual teacher. My goal is to simply share the Scriptures I found with you so that YOU can KNOW who you ARE in Christ.

On an interesting note, my intention was to title this entire book "Who Do You Think You Are?" Upon searching the Internet, I discovered a pastor named Mark Driscoll who studied Ephesians, authored a book by that title. So, I decided not to title this book the same.

Everything you DO flows out of WHO you THINK you ARE.

And speaking of THINKING, here are a few Scriptures on that subject:

Man is spirit, soul and body.

Spirit – We are "still-born" when we enter this earth. We inherit the sin nature just like we inherit our nationality. For example, my wife will always have Italian blood. She can't change that. When you come to know God and He places his Holy Spirit inside you, you become utterly clean, saved, redeemed, set free and everything else that is listed below.

In Christ, you are all that Scripture says you are.

Soul – Your soul is your **mind, will** and **emotion**. As the Holy Spirit is activated in your life, He cleanses your soul. It is a sanctification process. This is why it is so important to put the clean, the pure and the positive into your mind.

As you renew your mind, your emotions get into check and God's will is done rather than yours.

Body – Your body has been trained by your soul (mind, will and emotion). Your soul is impacted by your spirit. When you have the Holy Spirit inside of you, you have two ways to live: "In Christ" or "in the flesh." "By the Spirit" or "in the flesh."

Even when you have the Holy Spirit inside you, it doesn't mean that you always activate Him (the Holy Spirit). You have a choice every moment to live "by the flesh" or "by the Spirit.".

Every moment you have the opportunity to take every thought captive to the obedience of Christ.

As you renew your mind through thinking and praying, and you continually allow the Holy Spirit to cleanse you, you become a different person – a sanctified person who acts differently than before.

Did you know that one of the FRUITS of the Holy Spirit is "self-control"? The result is that you DO things differently because you have BEcome a different person.

Philippians 4:6-8 says: "Be anxious for nothing, but in everything by prayer and supplication with thanksgiving let your requests be made known to God. And the peace of God which surpasses all comprehension, shall guard your hearts and your *minds* in Christ Jesus. Finally brethren whatever is true, whatever is honorable, whatever is right, whatever is pure, whatever is lovely, whatever is of good repute, if there is any excellence and if anything worthy of praise, *let your mind dwell on these things.*

Romans 12:2 says "And do not be conformed to this world, but *be transformed by the renewing of your mind*, that you may prove what the will of God is, that which is good and acceptable and perfect.

"We have the mind of Christ." - 1 Corinthians 2:16b

Finally, 1 Corinthians 14:20 says "Brethren, do not be children in your thinking; yet in evil be infants, but in your thinking be mature."

The last chapter of my first book, *7 Secrets of a Phenomenal L.I.F.E,* is simply "I AM" because God called Himself "I AM." Jesus said, "Before Abraham was, I AM."

Now the I AM is IN YOU! That, my friend, is the mystery of knowing

Christ, the only Son of the only God. So, if you are a believer in Christ, you can put "I AM" before each of the Scriptures below. For example, when it says "Free," say "I AM Free!"

Here are the Scriptures I found for you. They are listed according to the order of the books of the New Testament, so you will see some of the words repeat in different chapters.

In Christ, YOU ARE...

THE CALLED

*among whom you also are **the called** of Jesus Christ;*

Romans 1:6

BELOVED – SAINTS

*to all who are **beloved** of God in Rome, called as **saints**: Grace to you and peace from God our Father and the Lord Jesus Christ.*

Romans 1:7

BLESSED and FORGIVEN

*"**BLESSED** are those whose lawless deeds have been **forgiven**, and whose sins*

have been covered.

*"**BLESSED** is the man whose sin the Lord will not take into account."*

Romans 4:7-8

HAVE PEACE

*1 we **have peace** with God through our Lord Jesus Christ,*

Romans 5:1

RECONCILED

*11 we have now received the **reconciliation**.*

Romans 5:11

FREED

*knowing this, that our old self was crucified with Him, in order that our body of sin might be done away with, so that we would no longer be slaves to sin; ⁷ for he who has died is **freed** from sin.*

Romans 6:6

UNDER GRACE

*¹⁴ For sin shall not be master over you, for you are not under law but **under grace.***

though you were slaves of sin,

Romans 6:14

OBEDIENT

*17 But thanks be to God that though you were slaves of sin, you became **obedient** from the heart to that form of teaching to which you were committed,*

Romans 6:17

FREED FROM SIN

*¹⁸ and having been **freed** from sin, you became slaves of righteousness.*

Romans 6:18

²⁰ For when you were slaves of sin, you were free in regard to righteousness.
²¹ Therefore what benefit were you then deriving from the things of which

*you are now ashamed? For the outcome of those things is death. ²² But now having been **freed** from sin and enslaved to God, you derive your benefit, resulting in sanctification, and the outcome, eternal life. ²³ For the wages of sin is death, but the **free gift** of God is eternal life in Christ Jesus our Lord.*

Romans 6:20-23

NOT CONDEMNED

SET FREE FROM THE LAW OF SIN AND DEATH

*1 Therefore there is now **no condemnation** for those who are in Christ Jesus. ² For the law of the Spirit of life in Christ Jesus has **set you free** from the law of sin and of death.*

Romans 8:1

HIS SPIRIT DWELLS IN YOU

*¹¹ But if the **Spirit of Him** who raised Jesus from the dead **dwells in you**, He who raised Christ Jesus from the dead will also give life to your mortal bodies through His Spirit who dwells in you.*

Romans 8:11

SONS

*⁶ Because you are **sons**, God has sent forth the Spirit of His Son into our hearts, crying, " Abba! Father!"*

Romans 8:15

CHILDREN OF GOD

*¹⁶ The Spirit Himself testifies with our spirit that we are **children of God**,*

HEIRS

Romans 8:16

HEIRS OF GOD – FELLOW HEIRS WITH CHRIST

*[17] and if children, heirs also, **heirs of God and fellow heirs with Christ**, if indeed we suffer with Him so that we may also be glorified with Him.*

Romans 8:16-17

PREDESTINED-CALLED- JUSTIFIED-GLORIFIED

*29 For those whom He foreknew, He also **predestined** to become conformed to the image of His Son, so that He would be the firstborn among many brethren; [30] and these whom He **predestined**, He also called; and these whom He **called**, He also **justified**; and these whom He justified, He also **glorified**.*

Romans 8:29-30

CONQUERER

*[37] But in all these things we overwhelmingly **conquer** through Him who loved us.*

Romans 8:37

SAVED

*[9] [that if you confess with your mouth Jesus as Lord, and believe in your heart that God raised Him from the dead, you will be **saved**;*

*[13] for "WHOEVER WILL CALL ON THE NAME OF THE LORD WILL BE **SAVED**."*

Romans 10:9 &13

FULL OF GOODNEWSS AND KNOWLEDGE

*[14] And concerning you, my brethren, I myself also am convinced that you yourselves are **full of goodness**, filled with all **knowledge** and able also to admonish one another*

Romans 15:14

SAINTS - SANCTIFIED

*² To the church of God which is at Corinth, to those who **have been sanctified** in Christ Jesus, **saints by calling**, with all who in every place call on the name of our Lord Jesus Christ, their Lord and ours:*

1 Corinthians 1:2

ENRICHED

*⁴ I thank my God always concerning you for the grace of God which was given you in Christ Jesus, ⁵ that in everything you were **enriched** in Him, in all speech and all knowledge,*

1 Corinthians 1:4

IN CHRIST

*³⁰ But by His doing you are **in Christ Jesus**,*

1 Corinthians 1:30

WE HAVE THE SPIRIT OF GOD

*¹² Now we have **received**, not the spirit of the world, but **the Spirit who is from God**, so that we may know the things freely given to us by God,*

1 Corinthians 2:12

WE HAVE THE MIND OF CHRIST

*¹⁶ For WHO HAS KNOWN THE MIND OF THE LORD, THAT HE WILL INSTRUCT HIM? But **we have the mind of Christ**.*

1 Corinthians 2:16

TEMPLE OF GOD - SPIRIT OF GOD DWELLS IN YOU

*[16] Do you not know that you are a **temple of God** and that the Spirit of God **dwells** in you?*

1 Corinthians 3:16

HOLY SPIRIT IS IN YOU

*[19] Or do you not know that your body is a temple **of the Holy Spirit who is in you**, whom you have from God, and that you are not your own?*

1 Corinthians 6:19

BOUGHT WITH A PRICE

[20] For you have been bought with a price: therefore glorify God in your body.

1 Corinthians 6:20

KNOWN BY GOD

*[3] but if anyone loves God, he is **known** by Him.*

1 Corinthians 8:3

AMBASSADORS

*[20] Therefore, we are **ambassadors** for Christ, as though God were making an appeal through us; we beg you on behalf of Christ, be reconciled to God. [21] He made Him who knew no sin to be sin on our behalf, so that we might become the righteousness of God in Him.*

1 Corinthians 8:20-21

SAVED

*[2] by which also you are **saved**, if you hold fast the word which I preached to you, unless you believed in vain.*

1 Corinthians 15:2

VICTORY OVER DEATH

*[57] but thanks be to God, who gives us the **victory** through our Lord Jesus Christ.*

1 Corinthians 15:57

SEALED BY THE SPIRIT

*[22] who also **sealed** us and gave us the Spirit in our hearts as a pledge.*

2 Corinthians 1:22

A NEW CREATURE

*[17] Therefore if anyone is in Christ, he is a **new creature**; the old things passed away; behold, new things have come.*

2 Corinthians 5:17

AMBASSADORS

*[20] Therefore, we are **ambassadors** for Christ,*

2 Corinthians 5:20

FREE

*It was for freedom that Christ set us **free**; therefore keep standing firm and do not be subject again to a yoke of slavery.*

Galatians 5:1

CRUCIFIED WITH CHRIST - CHRIST LIVES IN ME

*[20] I have been **crucified** with Christ; and it is no longer I who live, but **Christ lives in me;** and the life which I now live in the flesh I live by faith in the Son of God, who loved me and gave Himself up for me.*

Galatians 2:20

BLESSED-CHOSEN-HOLY-BLAMELESS-PREDESTINED-GRACE FREELY BESTOWED ON US - REDEMPTION- FORGIVENESS

*³ Blessed be the God and Father of our Lord Jesus Christ, who has **blessed** us with every spiritual blessing in the heavenly places in Christ, ⁴ just as He **chose** us in Him before the foundation of the world, that we would be **holy** and **blameless** before Him. In love ⁵ He **predestined** us to adoption as sons through Jesus Christ to Himself, according to the kind intention of His will, ⁶ to the praise of the glory of **His grace, which He freely bestowed** on us in the Beloved. ⁷ In Him we have **redemption** through His blood, the **forgiveness** of our trespasses, according to the riches of His grace ⁸ which He lavished on us. In all wisdom and insight ⁹ He made known to us the mystery of His will, according to His kind intention which He purposed in Him*

Ephesians 1:3-9

OBTAINED AN INHERITANCE

*In Him ¹¹ also we have obtained an **inheritance**, having been predestined according to His purpose who works all things after the counsel of His will, ¹² to the end that we who were the first to hope in Christ would be to the praise of His glory.*

Ephesians 1:11-12

ALIVE IN CHRIST

1 And you <u>were</u> dead in your trespasses and sins, ² in which you <u>formerly</u> walked according to the course of this world, according to the prince of the power of the air, of the spirit that is now working in the sons of disobedience. ³ Among them we too all formerly lived in the lusts of our flesh, indulging the desires of the flesh and of the mind, and <u>were</u> by nature children of wrath, even as the rest. ⁴ But God, being rich in mercy, because of His great love with which He loved us, ⁵ even when we were dead in our transgressions, made us **alive** together with Christ (by grace you have been saved),

Ephesians 2:1-5

RAISED UP, SEATED WITH HIM

6 and raised us up with Him, and seated us with Him in the heavenly places in Christ Jesus

Ephesians 2:6

NEAR TO GOD

*[13] But now in Christ Jesus you who formerly were far off have been **brought near** by the blood of Christ.*

Ephesians 2:13

WE HAVE ACCESS TO HIM

[18] for through Him we both have our access in one Spirit to the Father.

Ephesians 2:18

FELLOW CITIZENS WITH THE SAINTS

*[19] So then you are no longer strangers and aliens, but you are **fellow citizens** with the saints, and are of God's household, [20] having been built on the foundation of the apostles and prophets, Christ Jesus Himself being the corner stone,*

Ephesians 2:19-20

HOLY TEMPLE - DWELLING OF GOD

*[21] in whom the whole building, being fitted together, is growing into a holy temple in the Lord, [22] in whom you also are being built together into a **dwelling of God** in the Spirit.*

Ephesians 2:21

STREGNTHENED

strengthened with all power, according to His glorious might, for the attaining of all steadfastness and patience;

Colossians 1:11

QUALIFIED FOR INHERITANCE

For the attaining of all steadfastness and patience; joyously [12] giving thanks to the Father, who has **qualified us to share in the inheritance** of the saints in Light.

Colossians 1:12

RESCUED AND TRANSFERRED

[13] For He **rescued** us from the domain of darkness, and **transferred** us to the kingdom of His beloved Son, [14] in whom we have redemption, the forgiveness of sins.

Colossians 1:13

RECONCILED

[21] And although you were formerly alienated and hostile in mind, engaged in evil deeds, [22] yet He has now **reconciled** you in His fleshly body through death, in order to present you before Him holy and blameless and beyond reproach

Colossians 1:21-22

CHRIST IN YOU

[27] to whom God willed to make known what is the riches of the glory of this mystery among the Gentiles, which is **Christ in you**, the hope of glory.

Colossians 1:27

HAVE RECIEVED CHRIST

*⁶ Therefore as you have **received Christ** Jesus the Lord,*

Colossians 2:6

MADE COMPLETE

*¹⁰ and in Him you have been made **complete**,*

Colossians 2:10

CIRCUMCISED

*¹¹ and in Him you were also **circumcised** with a circumcision made without hands, in the removal of the body of the flesh by the circumcision of Christ;*

Colossians 2:11

BURIED WITH HIM - RAISED UP

*¹² having been **buried** with Him in baptism, in which you were also **raised up** with Him through faith in the working of God, who raised Him from the dead.*

Colossians 2:12

ALIVE - FORGIVEN

*¹³ When you were dead in your transgressions and the uncircumcision of your flesh, He made you **alive** together with Him, having **forgiven** us all our transgressions,*

Colossians 2:13

RAISED UP - WHERE CHRIST IS

*Therefore if you have been **raised up** with Christ, keep seeking the things above, where Christ is, seated at the right hand of God.*

Colossians 3:1

HAVE DIED

*³ For you **have died** and your life is hidden with Christ in God. ⁴ When Christ, who is our life, is revealed, then you also will be revealed with Him in glory.*

Colossians 3:3

SAVED

*⁵ He **saved** us, not on the basis of deeds which we have done in righteousness, but according to His mercy, by the washing of regeneration and renewing by the Holy Spirit, ⁶ whom He poured out upon us richly through Jesus Christ our Savior,*

Titus 3:5

JUSTIFIED -HEIRS

⁷ so that being **justified** by His grace we would be made **heirs** according to *the* hope of eternal life.

Titus 3:7

PARTAKERS OF A HEAVENLY CALLING

Therefore, holy brethren, **partakers** of a heavenly calling,

Hebrews 3:1

GOD'S HOUSE

*⁶ but Christ was faithful as a Son over His house— **whose house we are,** if we hold fast our confidence and the boast of our hope firm until the end.*

Hebrews 3:6

PARTAKERS OF CHRIST

*[14] For we have become **partakers of Christ**, if we hold fast the beginning of our assurance firm until the end,*

Hebrews 3:14

CLEANSED CONSCIENCE

*[14] how much more will the blood of Christ, who through the eternal Spirit offered Himself without blemish to God, **cleanse your conscience** from dead works to serve the living God?*

Hebrews 9:14

ETERNAL INHERITANCE

*Those who have been called may receive the promise of the **eternal inheritance**.*

Hebrews 9:15

CHOSEN

*Who are **chosen** according to the foreknowledge of God the Father, by the sanctifying work of the Spirit, to obey Jesus Christ and be sprinkled with His blood: May grace and peace be yours in the fullest measure*

1 Peter 1:1-2

BORN AGAIN

*[3] Blessed be the God and Father of our Lord Jesus Christ, who according to His great mercy has caused us to be **born again** to a living hope through the resurrection of Jesus Christ from the dead*

1 Peter 1:3

PROTECTED

*Who are **protected** by the power of God through faith for a salvation ready to be revealed in the last time.*

1 Peter 1:5

BORN AGAIN

*For you have been **born again** not of seed which is perishable but imperishable, that is, through the living and enduring word of God.*

1 Peter 1:23

LIVING STONES

*⁵ you also, as **living stones,** are being built up as a spiritual house for a holy priesthood, to offer up spiritual sacrifices acceptable to God through Jesus Christ.*

1 Peter 2:5

A CHOSEN RACE - A ROYAL PRIESTHOOD - A HOLY NATION

*But you are **A CHOSEN RACE**, A **royal** **PRIESTHOOD**, A **HOLY NATION**, A PEOPLE FOR God's OWN POSSESSION, so that you may proclaim the excellencies of Him who has called you out of darkness into His marvelous light; ¹⁰ for you once were NOT A PEOPLE, but now you are THE PEOPLE OF GOD; you had NOT RECEIVED MERCY, but now you have RECEIVED MERCY.*

1 Peter 2:9

HAVE EVERYTHING PERTAINING TO LIFE AND GODLINESS

³ seeing that His divine power has granted to us everything pertaining to life and godliness, through the true knowledge of Him who called us by His own glory and excellence.

2 Peter 1:3

PARTAKERS OF THE DIVINE NATURE

⁴ For by these He has granted to us His precious and magnificent promises, so that by them you may become partakers of the divine nature, having escaped the corruption that is in the world by lust.

2 Peter 1:4

CHILDREN OF GOD

See how great a love the Father has bestowed on us, that we would be called **children of God***; and such we are. For this reason the world does not know us, because it did not know Him. ² Beloved, now we are* **children of God***, and it has not appeared as yet what we will be. We know that when He appears, we will be like Him, because we will see Him just as He is.*

1 John 1-2

CPSIA information can be obtained at www.ICGtesting.com
Printed in the USA
BVOW03s2114251114

376768BV00007B/57/P